IMPRINT

Bibliographic information of the German National Library: The German National Library catalogs this publication in the German National Bibliography. Detailed bibliographic data can be accessed online at www.dnb.de. All rights of distribution, including excerpts, reprinting, photomechanical reproduction, and utilization in databases or similar institutions, are reserved.

Publisher: BoD · Books on Demand GmbH, Überseering 33, 22297 Hamburg, bod@bod.de.
Print: Libri Plureos GmbH, Friedensallee 273, 22763 Hamburg

ISBN: 978-3-8192-0891-1
(3. Auflage)

DEDICATION

For all survivors of violence who continue to carry light within them despite the darkness. Your courage and strength are an inspiration to us all.

THE AUTHOR

Verena Arps-Roelle is the founder of the initiative "act & protect® – AGAINST SEXUALIZED VIOLENCE." As an activist and expert, she advocates for a comprehensive approach to addressing sexualized violence. Her focus includes (entertainment) sexism, stereotypes, and victim blaming. Verena uses her personal experience as a survivor of sexualized violence to convey preventive and intervention measures that are practical and sustainable. She is committed to supporting other activists, institutions, and campaigns for societal and political change. As a consultant and trainer of the "act & protect® Academy," which she co-founded with Sebastian Arps, she supports companies, NGOs, associations, educational institutions, and individuals. Verena also certifies organizations with the "act & protect® Seal." As a speaker, she is known for her precise, compelling, and constructive presentations.

Learn more about Verena and her work at:

www.actandprotect.de
www.elementartraining.de/actandprotect

THE CO-AUTHOR

Sebastian Arps is an expert in (neuro-)communication, a sociologist, and a business psychologist. As the owner of Elementartraining, he supports companies and individuals through transformative processes. His work is characterized by a creative and constructive approach that fosters lasting change on both business and personal levels. With his deep understanding of structures and needs, he critically examines existing processes to help organizations and people recognize and break entrenched patterns. Sebastian's work is based on the four elements of personality: perception, emotion, cognition, and behavior - elements that only function effectively together. Many of the methods presented in this book were developed and refined by Sebastian for the act & protect® Academy and have been successfully implemented in practice. In 2024, Sebastian co-initiated the "Together for Democracy" alliance with Verena Arps-Roelle, advocating for democratic values, including in corporate settings.

Learn more about Sebastian and his work at:

www.elementartraining.de
www.gemeinsamfuerdemokratie.com

CURRENT CAMPAIGNS

Our non-profit work also includes drafting and publishing petitions on change.org and to the German Bundestag. We use these petitions to highlight legal gaps, societal issues, and necessary changes, bringing them into political discourse. Below is an overview of our current petitions (as of January 2025).

LEGAL RECOGNITION OF CATCALLING AS A CRIMINAL OFFENSE

In Germany, "sexual harassment" is currently only recognized as such if physical contact occurs (as of November 2020). Many European countries, such as France, Belgium, the Netherlands, Spain, and Portugal, have already criminalized catcalling, defined as sexually suggestive calling, talking, whistling, or gesturing toward a person in public spaces. Our demand to include catcalling as an independent criminal offense in German law is part of the leading petition PET 4-20-07-49121-003699, currently under review by the German Bundestag.

MORE PROTECTION IN ADVERTISING

This petition opposes sexualized depictions in advertising and media—both online and offline—particularly in relation to content targeting children and adolescents. The aim is to prevent discriminatory stereotypes and self-image distortions through education, competency development, and interdisciplinary training. A key focus is combating sexualized advertising and its misuse in the dark web through deepfakes (AI-manipulated media) and non-nudes (sexually suggestive images of non-nude individuals). This petition, ID 139418, is currently under review by the German Bundestag and has been undergoing a final geo-review by the state parliaments since January 2025.

CHILD- AND SURVIVOR-CENTERED JUSTICE

Supporting survivors requires legal proceedings adapted to their age and needs. This includes video interrogations, qualified trust persons, interdisciplinary collaboration among stakeholders, and binding quality standards. The Scandinavian Barnahus model serves as an inspiration. This petition, ID 139212, is under final review by the petitions committees of state parliaments sincef all 2024.

STOP ENTERTAINMENT SEXISM AND SEXUALIZED VIOLENCE IN REALITY TV

Protecting participants and audiences from sexist and abusive content in reality TV formats requires safe conditions. This petition aims to sanction boundary-crossing behavior, improve the media's handling of sensitive topics, and protect all involved. Submitted to the German Bundestag and the state parliament of North Rhine-Westphalia under ID 167903, it has also been forwarded to the Broadcasting Commission of the Minister Presidents and the state media authorities for evaluation.

PROLOGUE

Sexualized violence is a pervasive problem, but it must not become normalized. It manifests in all sociocultural and structural contexts: families, clubs, sports, social networks, advertising, media, schools, and workplaces. And in the workplace, it affects more people than commonly assumed.

In this book, we focus primarily on the example of Germany. However, we also draw comparisons with other countries, incorporating studies and additional insights. This is not a problem unique to Germany; it is a global issue. Across the world, we see similar patterns, numbers, data, and facts regarding sexualized violence. The impact and prevalence of this issue are evident in various sociocultural and structural contexts everywhere, emphasizing the need for a broader, international perspective on tackling it.

This book takes an in-depth look at the issue by following three essential steps toward violence-free workplace cultures:

1. See it

Understanding its definitions, forms, and dynamics. We reveal myths and misconceptions, clarify when sexualized violence begins, and discuss its personal, societal, and corporate impacts.

2. Name it

Examining its consequences, preventive measures, and appropriate interventions. We empower individuals and organizations to take responsibility and recognize their privileges and boundaries.

3. Stop it

Providing practical strategies for setting boundaries clearly and constructively. From survivors to allies to perpetrators—everyone benefits from acknowledging, addressing, and ending sexualized violence.

In doing so, we adhere to the principle that non-violence must not be associated with pigeonholing, general suspicion or mistrust.
Instead, we strive for a transparent, appreciative, inclusive and productive working culture - a culture that offers clear and constructive ways of dealing with sexualized violence.

Be a cactus.

In this book, you will encounter our cactus symbol. The cactus serves as a reminder to recognize and use your own strengths: Extend your spines, set boundaries, and defend yourself and others confidently.

The cactus symbol signals methods and approaches that help act decisively and respectfully in difficult situations. It is meant to encourage you to extend your individual spines, poke, and assert yourself. And to be more cactus.

CONTENT NOTICE

This book provides a comprehensive insight into the sensitive topic of "Sexualized Violence in the Workplace." It is not intended as legal advice or therapeutic support. Instead, it serves as an in-depth exploration of the various facets of sexualized violence, its impacts, and preventive and interventive measures within the work context.

As a reader, you will gain an understanding of the different forms of sexualized violence and how to categorize them. You will be equipped with knowledge, encouragement, and concrete action options. The content covers a broad range, from general information to legal and ethical aspects, and includes detailed statistics and facts. At the same time, we offer diverse impulses for support and effective empowerment. Our goal is to strengthen you mentally, professionally, and cognitively so that you can set, defend, and maintain your boundaries in the future in a safe, conscious, and unequivocal manner.

This book contains information about sexualized violence that may be retraumatizing or triggering for some readers. If you are personally affected and need support, please contact a professional counseling service near you or one of the help organizations listed at the end of the book under "Important Contacts."

The terms used, such as perpetrator, perpetrating party, affected person, victim, accused, and offender, are not used in a legal context in this book but within the framework of sexualized violence.

In legal texts and guidelines, the term "sexual harassment" is often used because it precisely and legally describes the various forms of violence characterized by sexual acts or assaults. This term is well-established in legal practice and allows for the specific classification and prosecution of crimes such as rape, sexual coercion, or sexual violence. The legal definitions of "sexual harassment" focus on physical and direct sexual assaults to hold perpetrators accountable and provide legal protection for the victims. However, in this book, we use the term "sexualized violence" from feminist language to do justice to the victims and provide a more comprehensive picture of violence. The term "sexualized violence" includes the physical dimension of sexual assaults but also encompasses emotional and psychological violence. This form of violence often appears in more subtle, less obvious manifestations, such as suggestive comments, discriminatory behaviors, or psychological manipulation—which also have significant impacts on the well-being of those involved. By using the term "sexualized violence," we want to acknowledge the multifaceted experiences and profound effects such violent experiences have. This broader perspective allows for the recognition and addressing of emotional and psychological dimensions of violence, which are not always sufficiently considered in many legal definitions. Our aim is to provide a more complete picture of sexualized violence in the workplace through more precise and comprehensive terminology. When we refer to the term "sexual harassment" in the context of laws, we place it in quotation marks.

In this book, we focus on the perspectives of people in mentally stable contexts. People with mental health conditions or in challenging psychological situations have specific needs as both victims and perpetrators, especially when it comes to sexualized violence and experiences. These situations require special considerations and support, which are not covered in this work. For comprehensive information and specialized support in such cases, we recommend consulting appropriate literature or specialized services. Through this focus, we aim to ensure that all people are adequately and respectfully supported and that we meet the diverse needs to avoid stigmatization and take into account the variety of human experiences and life realities.

We primarily refer to existing general conditions in Germany in this book. However, to enrich the discussion and provide a broader perspective, we also draw comparisons with other countries around the world.

Women* and Men*

Im In the spirit of inclusivity and sensitivity, we use the term "women" for all individuals who identify with the female gender or non-binary identities (i.e., people who do not feel like a man or woman, whose gender identity includes male and/or female aspects, lies somewhere in between, or is completely outside these categories) and "men" for all individuals who identify with the male gender or non-binary identities. In this book, we refrain from using the gender asterisk for the terms "man/men" and "woman/women" in order to create a space that respectfully and comprehensively represents the diversity of people in our society and their individual experiences while keeping the reading flow as smooth as possible.

This book does not claim to be comprehensive. The topic of sexualized violence is a constantly evolving field. Moral views change, new research is conducted, current studies are published, and laws are continuously updated. This is also why the book is designed so that each chapter can be read independently. This structure allows you to engage with the different topics individually and flexibly, diving deeper as needed. Through this modular approach, we foster a tailored reading experience that allows you to focus on the content most relevant to you.

Publishing through Books on Demand (BoD) is a conscious decision for us. Our goal is not to achieve high margins but to reach as many people as possible and offer our methods at fair prices. We want to ensure that our books are accessible to a wide audience and that potential readers are not deterred by excessive costs. At the same time, it is important to us to retain content control to ensure that our message remains unaltered.

We wish you exciting „I see!" moments, enriching knowledge deepening, and inspiring encouragement!

Verena Arps-Roelle & Sebastian Arps

CONTENT

NAME IT

STOP IT

INTRODUCTION

THROUGH TIME
THE HISTORY

The history of sexualized violence in the workplace in Germany and worldwide is long, complex, and distressing. For centuries, individuals have been exposed to sexualized violence in various forms at their workplaces. This affected both men and women, as well as individuals perceived as female, male, and non-binary.

In the following pages, we will explore the last few centuries to provide an impression of the variety and severity of these experiences.

These pages offer an initial glimpse into the complexity of the topic, which reveals even more facets across all eras upon closer examination.

SEXUALIZED VIOLENCE AGAINST WOMEN: THROUGH THE CENTURIES

Women have been, and continue to be, exposed to sexualized violence in the workplace—a problem that spans throughout history. In many cultures and periods, women were subjected not only to human trafficking and economic exploitation but also to sexual assault. This violence served as a means of control, degradation, and the exertion of power.

Access to education and professional opportunities for girls and women was severely restricted across many eras. They were often limited to certain roles, shaped by gender-specific norms and hierarchies. These disadvantages increased their vulnerability to sexualized violence, which in turn led to health problems, marginalization, job loss, poverty, and even suicide. In earlier centuries, particularly in smaller towns and villages, many women were heavily dependent on the community. There was often a culture of silence or the belief that such assaults were the inevitable lot of women.

Due to poverty, the loss of the male head of the household, or a lack of employment opportunities, many women were forced into prostitution. They were often controlled by pimps who used violence to force them into prostitution or prevent them from leaving. Clients also frequently exercised violence. The societal stigma intensified their isolation and made it difficult for them to find help—a situation that still persists in some aspects today.

Until the 18th century, women were often persecuted, tortured, and killed under the pretext of witchcraft—especially those who worked as midwives or healers and deviated from normative expectations.
Even during the Industrial Revolution in the 19th century, women's conditions did not improve. Despite their increasing

presence in factories and male-dominated professions, they remained unprotected from sexualized violence. Instead, the increasing participation of women in the labor market was associated with their segregation into poorly paid jobs. Women were seen as "cheap labor," which in turn facilitated sexualized violence in all its forms.

At the beginning of the 20th century, the German Civil Code (BGB) stipulated that women, especially married women, were subject to numerous legal restrictions. They needed their husband's consent to take up paid work. This regulation was based on the concept of gender roles, which saw the man as the primary breadwinner and the woman as the housewife and mother. Traditional male control within the family was threatened by working women, often leading to violence, power struggles, and dominant behaviors.

Women faced social pressure to stay at home, while the economic pressure to support themselves was great. This was a difficult situation, especially for single, divorced, and widowed women, who had to take on multiple risks. Court documents from this period show that many female employees were abused by their male employers.

In the early industrial period, society made no distinction between working women, prostitutes, and criminal groups. This was due to several factors: women from poor families had to work, yet it was unusual for women to work outside the home. Both prostitutes and paid workers were seen as escaping patriarchal control, which was intended to be reclaimed through sexualized violence. It made no difference whether women were selling their labor or sexual services.

At this time, responses from women to sexualized violence in the workplace can be divided into individual and collective reactions. Some women viewed sexual violence and harassment as a personal problem or bad luck. Others saw it as a social issue and responded collectively by joining unions and other organizations to secure legal protection.

During World War I and World War II, women worked to fill the gaps left by men who were sent to the front lines. They took up jobs in factories, agriculture, and many other areas that had previously been dominated by men. In addition to their work, they helped rebuild society and the economy after the war. However, after World War II, as men returned from the front lines and from prisoner-of-war camps, society's attitudes toward women shifted once again. The focus returned to traditional gender roles. Women were expected to resume the role of housewife and mother, concentrating on household duties, child-rearing, and supporting their partners. Many societal and political forces pushed for men to reclaim their jobs and experience the "normalcy" they had lost during the war. This return to traditional role models, alongside existing societal norms and legal frameworks, discouraged many women from continuing their careers or pursuing new professional opportunities.

Until 1957, § 1356 of the German Civil Code (BGB) stipulated that women were generally subordinated to their husbands in household and child-rearing matters and could only work with their husband's consent. The decisive change came with the reform of marriage and family law: from 1957 onwards, women no longer needed their husband's explicit permission to work. Nevertheless, the idea that women were primarily responsible for the household and supporting their husbands remained deeply ingrained.

It was not until the 1960s that these attitudes began to gradually change. Women gained increasing access to a broader range of professions and career opportunities.

In the 1960s and 1970s, women worldwide fought for equal rights and against sexualized violence, including in the workplace. The feminist movement helped raise awareness of the need for reforms. Many countries introduced laws to combat various forms of sexualized violence and establish protective measures for victims.

In the 1970s, the principle of equality between men and women was more strongly enshrined in law, particularly through amendments to the Basic Law. Article 3 now guaranteed equality between men and women, and from that point on, women no longer needed their spouse's consent to work.

The #MeToo movement, initiated by activist Tarana Burke in 2006 and globally popularized by actress Alyssa Milano in 2017, brought the issue back into the spotlight. Under the hashtag #MeToo, countless women shared their experiences of sexualized violence and "sexual harassment," exposing the extent of the problem and leading to calls for comprehensive change.
Despite these advances, women still experience sexualized violence in the workplace today.

SEXUALIZED VIOLENCE AGAINST MEN: A TABOO TOPIC

Although sexualized violence against men in the workplace is less well-documented, it nevertheless existed. Historical examples show that men became victims in various contexts. Men were victims of sexual violence in the context of human trafficking, used as a means of gratification, suppression, and control.

In earlier centuries, men as serfs were in a strong dependency relationship with a landowner. Even as servants or household employees, they faced dependence on their employers, which facilitated sexual exploitation due to the power imbalance.

Even in monastic or other religious institutions, male novices or monks were subjected to sexual assault by higher-ranking members of the community. These abuses were often promoted by the authority of the perpetrators within the institution and were more frequently covered up to protect the institution's reputation and the sanctity of the perpetrators.

In seafaring, particularly during long voyages, men were exposed to assaults. The isolated environment and strict hierarchies made it difficult to escape or resist such violations.

Particularly in male-dominated workplaces, abuse of power and harassment occurred. In such contexts, sexualized violence was used as a means of intimidation or to demonstrate dominance. Gender stereotypes and social norms often led men to hesitate (and still do today) in discussing their experiences or seeking help-out of fear of being perceived as weak, unmanly, or stigmatized.

In military contexts, particularly during wartime, soldiers or prisoners of war experienced sexual violence as torture, to humiliate or demonstrate power, and to inflict psychological damage. Historical records, such as reports on prisoners of war, often contain references to such mistreatment.

Until the year 2000, gay and bisexual Bundeswehr soldiers were treated unfairly and disadvantaged in military service, as they were considered a security risk. Studies, such as "Taboo and Tolerance" by the Center for Military History and Social Sciences of the Bundeswehr from 2019[1], show that men in various military contexts were affected by sexualized violence.

What has persisted throughout history is the idea that men must always be strong, unshakable, and honorable. These stereotypes are a subtle yet profound form of sexualized violence that continues to this day.

SEXUALIZED VIOLENCE AGAINST LGBTQIA+ PERSONS: HARD TO ENDURE

The LGBTQIA+ community has a long history of sexualized violence in the workplace. In many societies, same-sex relationships and other forms of queer identities were heavily stigmatized and criminalized. In Europe, homosexual relationships were often met with harsh penalties such as imprisonment, forced labor, or even the death penalty. LGBTQIA+ individuals lived in constant fear of persecution, concealed their identities, and lived in secrecy—significantly limiting their professional opportunities. Being openly queer often meant social exclusion and the loss of jobs.
From the late 19th century to the mid-20th century, some Western countries began to cautiously move towards decriminalization, while others continued to enforce strict laws. These not only led to criminal penalties but also had devastating effects on the victims' professional existence. Many lost their jobs or were forced to keep their sexual orientation secret to avoid professional disadvantages.

In Germany, for example, § 175[2], which criminalized sexual acts between men, was applied during the Imperial era and the Weimar Republic, and was tightened under Nazi Germany. LGBTQIA+ individuals were persecuted, stigmatized with the "pink triangle," sent to concentration camps, and murdered.

In the German Democratic Republic (GDR), the provision was only applied in a mitigated form between 1957 and 1968 and was subsequently removed from the Criminal Code. In the Federal Republic of Germany (FRG), the law was only amended in 1969: homosexual acts between adult men over the age of 21 were made unpunishable. It was not until 1994 that the Bundestag decided to finally abolish Section 175. In 2002, the German Bundestag repealed the sentences passed during the National Socialist era. However, it was not until July 22, 2017 that all judgments after 1945 were also repealed. Since March 2019, there has been an additional directive that enables all persecuted members of the LGBTQIA+ community to apply for one-off compensation for negative effects such as job loss.

Since then, comprehensive national and international anti-discrimination laws have been enacted to protect LGBTQIA+ people in the workplace. These often include provisions that prohibit discrimination on the basis of sexual orientation and gender identity and are intended to ensure equal access to employment opportunities. In addition, there are increased efforts towards equality and inclusion. However, the situation varies greatly around the world: in some countries there are far-reaching protective rights and social acceptance, while in other countries LGBTQIA+ people continue to be prosecuted or face social discrimination. These different legal frameworks have a significant impact on the professional opportunities and working lives of LGBTQIA+ people.

People from this community continue to frequently experience harassment, abuse and discrimination due to their sexual orientation, gender identity or gender expression, including in Germany. These experiences occur particularly in professional fields that are characterized by traditional gender roles and heteronormative ideas. One striking example is the "Lavender Scare"[3] in the USA during the 1950s: homosexual civil servants were persecuted and dismissed because their sexual orientation was falsely associated with a possible link to communism in the Soviet Union, making them a security risk. This targeted discrimination led to systematic persecution and public humiliation.

In the arts and entertainment industry, LGBTQIA+ people have also experienced significant discrimination and abuse over time - they have been exploited, persecuted and ostracized.

In many military and police institutions, discrimination against LGBTQIA+ people was widespread. These organizations, which are often highly hierarchical and tradition-bound, excluded or harassed individuals from the LGBTQIA+ community.

It is particularly important to recognize the specific challenges that the LGBTQIA+ community has faced and continues to face in relation to sexualized violence in the workplace and to take appropriate measures to prevent and support them.

SEXUALIZED VIOLENCE:
AN EVERYDAY PHENOMENON

DScandals and reports have revealed the extent of the issue, leading to broader debate and heightened awareness. It is now recognized that sexualized violence in work relationships can be perpetrated not only by superiors or colleagues but also by customers, clients, business partners, or others.

This realization has been an important step forward, as it broadens the understanding of power dynamics and the many different settings in which violations can occur. It underscores that sexualized violence is not limited to hierarchical structures within companies—it can just as easily happen in lateral or external relationships, often made more complex by dependencies or economic pressures.

Sexualized violence at work can take many forms, some of which are overt and easily identified, while others are subtle and insidious. It may include physical assault, sexually explicit comments, suggestive gestures, invasive personal questions, persistent unwelcome attention, digital harassment such as inappropriate messages or image sharing, or the coercive misuse of authority. The boundaries are often fluid, and what might at first appear as a "harmless joke" can be deeply degrading, especially when repeated or tolerated in a broader culture of silence or denial.

Victims of such violence come from all genders and backgrounds. They may be young or experienced, introverted or outspoken. What unites many of them is the inner conflict they experience: Should they speak out and risk professional backlash, social isolation, or not being believed? Or should they endure the situation in silence, often at the cost of their well-being and mental health? This dilemma highlights one of the most dangerous aspects of sexualized violence in the workplace: its tendency to be trivialized, ignored, or even normalized within professional cultures that prioritize performance, profit, or hierarchy over the dignity and safety of individuals.

Sexualized violence in the workplace is, therefore, not a private issue or an isolated incident—it is a structural and societal problem. It must be addressed comprehensively, regardless of gender or gender identity. Everyone has the right to work in an environment free from violence. That right is not a privilege, nor a bonus for those in "safe" professions or high-ranking positions—it is a fundamental human right that must be guaranteed across all sectors, hierarchies, and industries. Creating a truly safe and respectful working environment demands more than written policies or mission statements. It requires a lived culture of accountability, where boundaries are respected, violations are consistently addressed, and affected individuals are supported without fear of stigmatization. This includes transparent reporting procedures, effective protection against retaliation, regular awareness and prevention trainings, and leadership that actively demonstrates zero tolerance for harassment or abuse.

Equally important is the role of bystanders—colleagues, teammates, supervisors—who have the power to intervene, to listen, to support, and to stand in solidarity with those affected. Bystander intervention is not about replacing legal mechanisms but about creating a culture where silence and inaction are no longer the norm. The more people learn to recognize signs of sexualized violence and understand their role in preventing it, the more resilient and respectful our workplaces become.
It is the responsibility of employers, trade unions, governments, and society as a whole to take appropriate measures to ensure

this right. Addressing sexualized violence is not an optional "extra" in modern workplace policy—it is an essential aspect of organizational health, social responsibility, and sustainable development.

Sexualized violence in the workplace is an everyday phenomenon that must no longer be accepted as such. Despite progress in awareness and increased legal protection against sexualized violence in the workplace, many people continue to be affected.

It's time to finally change this!

SEE

IT

CHAPTER 1

BEHIND THE CURTAIN
SEXUALIZED VIOLENCE AT WORK TODAY

Sexualized Violence in the Workplace Today
If you think that assaults only occur in dark alleys or shady corners, unfortunately, you are mistaken.

The reality is that sexualized violence occurs in all socio-cultural and structural environments, as well as across age groups. It can happen in families, clubs, sports facilities, social networks, advertising, media, schools, and indeed also in companies and organizations.

Yes, even in the workplace, there are suggestive comments, sexual abuse, and structural discrimination.

Sexualized violence is a form of exerting power, manifested through non-consensual sexual acts, suggestive remarks, looks, insults or humiliations, inappropriate touching, and even rape. It is not about consensual (mutual) sexual acts but about crossing boundaries and abuse that involve a violent component. It also concerns discrimination in the form of structural disadvantage, normative roles, and outdated gender stereotypes. The German General Equal Treatment Act[4] refers to "sexual harassment" when:

> *"[...] an unwanted, sexually determined behavior, which also includes unwanted sexual acts and requests for these, sexually determined physical touches, remarks of a sexual nature, as well as unwanted displays and visible attachment of pornographic representations, is intended or has the effect of violating the dignity of the person concerned, especially when an environment characterized by intimidation, hostility, humiliation, degradation, or insults is created."*

Such behaviors violate the dignity of the person involved by insulting, degrading, or shaming them. It does not matter whether this insult was intentional; what matters is how the person affected feels about it. Sexualized violence is facilitated by dependencies, power structures, feelings of loyalty, and inequalities. In a world where abuse of power and inequality are commonplace, it is all the more important that we address the issue of sexualized violence. Only in this way can we learn how to protect ourselves and others, stop, prevent, and ideally eliminate these actions.

THE DARK REALITY: DEFINITIONS AND FORMS

Sexualized violence in the workplace is not a trivial offense but a serious problem. The term refers to any form of unwanted sexual behavior that harasses, threatens, or humiliates a person at the workplace. The consequences can be severe, ranging from psychological strain and stress to long-term effects on physical and emotional health. Only by having a precise definition and awareness of this issue can we effectively combat sexualized violence in all its forms.

Sexual Harassment

includes any sexualized and unwanted behavior. This includes not only verbal and physical harassment, such as sexual comments, sexual innuendos or threats, sexual blackmail, or unwanted touching, but also non-verbal forms such as suggestive looks or the showing of pornographic images, as well as inappropriate advances.

According to a 2022 study by the Federal Anti-Discrimination Agency[5] on dealing with sexual harassment in the workplace, 62% of respondents experienced harassment in the form of sexualized comments, 44% reported unwanted looks, gestures, or catcalling, and 26% experienced unwanted touches. 9% of respondents, about one in eleven employed individuals, were affected by "sexual harassment" in the workplace. Women experienced "sexual harassment" significantly more often at 13% compared to men (5%). In the aviation industry, the results are even more striking. In a survey by the Independent Flight Attendant Organization (UFO) in 2018 and 2019, around 52% of female respondents reported having been victims of "sexual harassment" at work, as well as 44% of male respondents and 75% of non-binary respondents. In 45% of the cases, the perpetrators were supervisors[6].

Sexual Coercion

involves forced sexual contact or sexual acts against a person's will, including rape or attempted rape.

According to a 2020 survey by the Bureau of Justice Statistics for victims[7] 7.8% of female respondents and 1.4% of male respondents experienced sexual coercion at work. Examples include supervisors threatening employees and forcing them into sexual acts or colleagues forcing kisses or touches against the victim's will.

Sexual Discrimination

refers to the verbal or non-verbal degradation of a person or group of people due to their gender affiliation and includes differential treatment based on gender or gender identity, especially in hiring, promotion, salary, working conditions, or other professional aspects.

The Gender Equality Index of the European Union from 2022[8] hows that women in the EU still earn on average 13% less than men. In Germany, the Gender Pay Gap (the difference between men's and women's wages) is 18%, putting Germany in fourth-to-last place in the EU comparison. This starkly demonstrates gender-specific discrimination regarding salary as a form of structural sexualized violence in the workplace. Women are often systematically paid less, passed over for promotions, or downgraded as unsuitable for traditionally male-dominated professions.

Stalking

is the repeated, unwanted following, harassing, or threatening of a person, including online stalking or cyber-stalking. More than one in ten people are affected by stalking at some point in their lives.

In 2019, according to the German Federal Criminal Police Office[9] there were 16,432 police-recorded incidents involving female victims and 3,772 involving male victims in Germany. The incidents included unwanted following, threatening, harassing, both offline and online - including in the workplace. The stalker came from the work environment in 9.1% of the cases and from professional contacts in 4.5% of the cases[10].

Gender Stereotypes and Sexism

Sexism refers to discriminatory attitudes or practices in which people are disadvantaged or favored due to their gender. While sexism can affect anyone, it predominantly targets women. Sexist assumptions about women and men manifest in gender stereotypes, which are prejudices or beliefs that assume one gender possesses certain characteristics or abilities that make it superior or inferior compared to the other gender. These stereotypes affect not only professional roles but also behavior, interests, and emotional expressions. For example, stereotypical assumptions might suggest that women are better suited for caregiving professions or that men require less emotional support. This hierarchical thinking can appear both consciously and hostilely, as well as unconsciously, through automated biases. Such assumptions affect how people are judged and treated based on their gender and often lead to discrimination.

They disadvantage individuals in accessing opportunities and resources and reinforce inequalities across various areas of life.

Vulnerability

People with disabilities, physical, mental, and cognitive challenges, as well as pronounced social and emotional needs, are at an increased risk of becoming victims of sexualized violence. Additionally, individuals who are subjected to intersectional discrimination are more likely to experience sexualized violence than others. Intersectional discrimination refers to the interaction of various forms of discrimination, such as racism, sexism, ableism, age discrimination, or LGBTQIA+ hostility. People who are discriminated against due to multiple characteristics often face an increased risk of sexualized violence because they encounter several dimensions and types of prejudice and discrimination that heighten their vulnerability. They may be less able to defend themselves against sexualized violence or talk about it due to their potentially dependent or vulnerable position in society. They can also be targeted by perpetrators who may believe they will offer less resistance. Moreover, people with pronounced social and emotional needs, such as those with low self-esteem or strong dependency behaviors, may more easily fall into hierarchical relationships that favor sexualized violence. Perpetrators exploit this need to exert power and control.

CASES:
THREE EXAMPLES

#1

Anna works in an office as a graphic designer. She is a passionate and talented employee who gets along well with her colleagues. Recently, however, she has noticed that a certain colleague, Peter, keeps making suggestive jokes and comments about her. Every day when Anna enters the room, Peter says things like: "Look, here comes our pretty little graphic genius. Hopefully, you won't distract us too much!" Or he makes comments about her appearance, saying: "Wow, you look especially sharp today. I can see why clients prefer working with you!" Anna feels uncomfortable and harassed by these comments. She tries to avoid Peter and ignore the issue. However, it is becoming increasingly difficult for her to cope with it. Peter's behavior negatively impacts her focus and productivity, as she constantly fears what Peter will say or do next.

#2

Christian works as a junior manager in a renowned corporation. During an informal meeting, his boss, Lisa, grabs his buttocks. Christian is shocked and feels used by this touch. He decides to speak to Lisa, politely but firmly asking her to refrain from such physical contact. But instead of taking his concerns seriously, Lisa dismisses him and labels him as a man who "shouldn't make such a big deal out of it." Lisa mocks Christian's feelings and his reaction, making him feel even more humiliated and discouraged. Determined to resolve the situation and not tolerate inappropriate behavior, Christian decides to report the incident to his direct superior. He describes what happened and makes it clear that he feels harassed and uncomfortable. His superior downplays the incident and even advises Christian to be pleased with the supposed compliment and use Lisa's apparent interest to further his career. The consequences of this situation are devastating for Christian. He feels sexually harassed, demeaned, and abandoned.

#3

Jaden has been working for several years as a sales associate in a large retail company. She is a dedicated and competent employee who builds great relationships with her customers. Jaden is also a transgender woman and is undergoing her transition. Jaden notices that her supervisor, since she shared this with her team, assigns her unusually often to tasks outside of customer-facing areas, such as inventory management. She realizes she is the only person on the team who is given these assignments. Over time, Jaden comes to realize that there is intent behind this. She feels excluded, disempowered, and deprived of the opportunity to advance in her career. And she doesn't know how to address this issue.

What do you feel when reading these examples?
Is this sexualized violence?

Yes!

Anna from the first example is a victim of sexualized violence in the form of comments, insinuations, and stereotypes.

Christian in the second example experiences unwanted physical contact and sexual objectification, followed by trivialization.

In the third example, Jaden experiences structural discrimination as a form of sexualized violence.

What unites them all is that they do not need to explicitly state the inappropriate behavior or the undesirability of a behavior, whether it occurs in the workplace or is related to it. It is assumed that the perpetrator knows what constitutes objectively unwanted behavior. After all, everyone should know what is negative and what is positive behavior. Unfortunately, the reality is different.

The causes of sexualized violence in the workplace are deeply rooted in our society and reflect established power dynamics, attempts at control, and dependencies.

How?

You will learn more in the following chapters. But let this much be said already: Each individual has shared responsibility. Everyone can contribute to creating a work environment where sexualized violence is not tolerated and where all people are respected and protected. Because:

Sexualized violence is not flirting.

Sexualized violence is not help.

Sexualized violence is not a joke.

Sexualized violence is not a compliment.

Sexualized violence is violence.

WHEN IS IT ENOUGH:
WHEN DOES SEXUALIZED VIOLENCE BEGIN?

Sexualized violence often begins much earlier than many people think. It is a insidious form of overreach that encompasses various aspects, violating people's dignity, freedom, will, and boundaries.

This violence is not only expressed in criminal acts but also in behaviors that are not punishable by law, which occur both in direct interaction and virtually and digitally in many forms.

Flirt oder assault?

Often, violence is equated only with physical violence. In fact, sexualized violence begins much earlier—even though many forms in everyday life are not punishable by law. Especially harassment is often trivialized and classified as less dangerous than it really is. Examples of this are supposedly "failed" flirting attempts.

And yes, flirting is not violence and is not prohibited in the workplace unless companies regulate this in their codes of conduct. However, flirting is based on mutual consent, while overreaching behavior occurs without the other person's consent.

But it doesn't end here.

Sexual comments, sexist jokes, and suggestive remarks find their place in meetings, in the office kitchen, or at parties. These forms of harassment are often subtle and easily overlooked or trivialized, but they significantly contribute to creating a hostile work environment. Inappropriate remarks do not lighten the atmosphere; rather, they disrupt the professional environment and undermine respect and equality. Even if such comments are often made under the guise of "fun" or "camaraderie," they cross personal integrity boundaries and cause others to feel uncomfortable or unprotected.

Sexualized violence can also be content-based. Unwanted suggestive, pornographic, objectifying, or sexualizing representations and texts - both analog and digital -are a serious issue, even in the workplace

FACES OF SEXUALIZED VIOLENCE: AT THE WORKPLACE

Sexualized violence at the workplace manifests in many ways and includes a range of problematic behaviors that are unwanted, inappropriate, intrusive, intimidating, and one-sided.

These behaviors are sexual, suggestive, ambiguous, stereotypical, gender- and sexuality-related:

Verbal

- Comments, remarks, or jokes
- Statements about clothing, appearance, or private life
- Questions about intimacy or relationships
- Outing a person
- Rumors or slander about sexual activities or relationships
- Requests for sexual acts
- Invitations for private dates
- Threats with sexual acts

Nonverbal

- Staring, gawking, whistle after („Catcalling")
- Gestures, movements, or signs
- Emails, chats, letters, text messages, photos, or videos
- Online harassment or cyberbullying
- Recording or sharing images or videos in intimate situations
- Posting or spreading pornographic materials or sexual images and texts

Physical

- Expose
- Seemingly accidental touches (e.g., patting, pinching, hugging, kissing)
- Physical closeness that does not maintain the intimate distance (about an arm's length)
- Forced sexual acts or overreach
- Manipulation to force sexual acts
- Pressuring someone to engage in, endure, or reciprocate a sexual act
- Rape

Structural

Sexualized violence also includes structural dimensions, such as discrimination based on gender and stereotypical ideas about gender roles. Gender-specific inequalities (Gender Gaps) show up in the Gender Pay Gap (pay disparities between men and women), the Gender Employment Gap (differences in employment participation between genders), and the Gender Data Gap (lack of gender-specific data). These gaps in gender equality exacerbate structural inequalities.

Isn't That a Bit Exaggerated?

No!

Sexualized violence in the workplace is not an exaggerated topic. On the contrary!

GENDER GAPS:
INJUSTICE BETWEEN THE GENDERS

Structural and gender-specific inequalities foster power imbalances. And power imbalances are a crucial factor in sexualized violence. For example, unequal pay structures can lead to employees, often women, having lower salaries and fewer promotion opportunities despite having the same competencies and positions. As a result, they are not only more likely to experience poverty but also at a higher risk of power abuse and dependency. Those who earn less are seen as less important, less powerful, and less valuable, which leads to devaluation, exploitation, and being used.

In 2023, the unadjusted Gender Pay Gap (difference in gross hourly earnings) in Germany[11] was 18%. Women earned an average of 4.46 euros less per hour than men. Around 60% of this gap is due to factors like industry affiliation and part-time work with often lower hourly wages. Men worked an average of 148 hours per month, while women worked 121 hours, which corresponds to an 18% reduction in working hours (Gender Hours Gap – difference in paid working hours per month).

In 2024, the unadjusted gender pay gap in the European Union averaged 13%. In Germany, this gap was 16%. Latvia had the largest gap at 19%, while Luxembourg reported a negative gender pay gap of -0.9%, meaning women earned more than men on average there.[12] Globally, the World Economic Forum estimates that it would take about 134 years to completely close the gender gap. This estimate accounts for factors like the underrepresentation of women in leadership positions and certain industries, as well as the unequal distribution of unpaid care work.[13] Despite some progress, the gender pay gap remains a significant issue both in Europe and worldwide. Initiatives such as promoting pay equality, transparent salary structures, and supporting women in leadership roles are crucial for further improvements.

And guess what, in which two professions do women worldwide earn significantly more than men?

Correct! As models and porn actresses

There are also disparities in employment participation: In 2022, 73% of women and 80.5% of men were employed, which results in a 9% Gender Employment Gap. The resulting Gender Gap in the Labor Market (indicator from average gross hourly earnings, number of paid working hours per month, and employment participation rate) reflects inequality in the labor market.
Such unequal employment conditions quickly put people in financial dependencies that make it difficult to report or act against harassment or discrimination. The fear of retaliation or job loss is too great and existentially threatening. This especially affects women, who find themselves in the so-called "part-time trap." This situation describes the often problematic circumstances of women who, due to care work (childcare, elderly care, family support, domestic care, and help among friends), often reduce their working hours. Such employment relationships, however, are often associated with fewer opportunities for promotion, less security, and less influence over working conditions. In these contexts, women are particularly vulnerable to harassment or discrimination and have fewer opportunities to defend themselves or seek support due to financial and family-organizational dependency.

While many companies promote such "family-friendly" part-time measures, they are often only tailored to the needs of women. Men who also need flexibility or entrepreneurial support often experience insufficient offers or stigmatization when they want or actually take advantage of such measures.

Another aspect of power inequality is the "glass ceiling." This metaphor describes the invisible barriers that make it difficult or even impossible for women and LGBTQIA+ individuals to rise to higher leadership levels, even though they are qualified. When they do reach higher positions, they are often underrepresented, particularly at the top levels of leadership. These structural obstacles lead to less influence on decision-making processes and, therefore, fewer opportunities to address discrimination and harassment. Most leadership positions are still held by men. In 2022, the relative proportion of women in leadership positions in the European Union (EU) was 38%. In 2023, only about one-third of leaders in Germany (28.7%) were women[14].

The maritime industry, for example, is still a male-dominated field - it wasn't until 1945 that the Maritime Professional Association lifted the ban on women in seafaring jobs. Ten years later, Annaliese Frieda Sparbier became the first woman to earn a German captain's license. It took another 30 years for a woman to stand at the helm, and even today, women at sea are rare. The International Maritime Organization (IMO) estimates that only 2.1% of crew members on board are women. In Germany, 6.3% of the crew is female[15]. Around 1,400 captains sail in Germany, with only 0.7% to 1% being women. The overrepresentation of male perspectives exacerbates the problems - not just in such extreme examples.

To counter this, quota regulations aim to promote a fairer distribution of genders in leadership positions. Quotas are intended to help bring more women into decision-making positions, balance power relations, and simultaneously benefit from the skills of the respective "quota women."
However, it is important that such measures are not merely symbolic in nature, in example subjected to "gender-washing," but also come with concrete changes in company culture and structures. Only if everyone has the same opportunities to as-

sert themselves at all levels of the company and be heard can an environment be created in which sexualized violence is effectively combated.

Otherwise, the low presence of women in leadership remains. The Global Gender Gap Report 2020 by the World Economic Forum[16] shows that the share of women in leadership positions worldwide is only 36%. In certain industries, such as technology or finance, this share is even lower. This is partly because women and men often choose different careers, which is due to gender-specific separations in the labor market. Women are often found in lower-paying jobs with fewer opportunities for advancement. Men, on the other hand, often have difficulty gaining access to occupations traditionally seen as "female" and asserting themselves in the long term against societal expectations.

Although more than one million women work in the typically male-dominated STEM professions (mathematics, IT, natural sciences, technology), according to the German Economic Institute in March 2020[17], this only corresponds to 15.3% of all employees in this field. The number of female STEM students has also been stagnating for years.

This underrepresentation of women is also evident in political decision-making positions. According to the Gender Statistics Database of the European Institute for Gender Equality (EIGE)[18], in September 2020, 86% of the presidency and prime minister positions in the European Union were held by men, and 69% of ministerial positions were occupied by men. In the European Parliament, the European Union Council (EU), and the European Commission, men made up 66% of higher leadership positions. Also, most EU bodies and institutions are led by men. Twenty years ago, this imbalance was even more pronounced: 100% of the heads of state and government of EU member states were men, and 90% of the bodies and institutions of the EU were led by men. Similarly, 86% of senior leadership positions in EU bodies and institutions were held by men.

Well, at least some progress to date. If we continue like this, we will achieve equal representation in about 70 years.

But these inequalities are not just a matter of fairness or a "Nice-to-Have," they are of vital importance. But these inequalities are not just a question of fairness or a nice-to-have, they are of vital importance.

For example, years of using crash test dummies designed according to male body measurements have led to women suffering significantly more injuries or even dying in car accidents. Newer generations of vehicles, which are also tested with dummies that conform to the female anatomy and are equipped with dual airbags, reduce the estimated fatality risk for women compared to men, according to a 2022 report by the NHTSA (National Highway Traffic Safety Administration)[19]. The estimated difference in the risk of death for female versus male front-row occupants is only 6.3% for 2010-2020 model year vehicles, compared to 18.3% for 1960-2009 model year vehicles. This difference decreases further to 2.9% for the latest model year vehicles (2015-2020). And now there are finally anatomically diverse crash test dummies for women, men and children.

Phew. It's about time.

But there is another area where the female perspective has been lacking: Life-threatening outcomes in drug development[20]. In most research, more male subjects are used than female subjects. Drugs are tested on men rather than women. In many medical fields, there is less data on women than on men - there is a gender data gap.

Why is that so?

Because additional markers have to be included for women, such as pregnancies, the difference before and after the menopause or the influence of the menstrual cycle.

So better without women then?
This means that the results obtained from studies conducted mainly with men are then transferred to women - regardless of their anatomical and hormonal characteristics. This leads to different results which, depending on gender, can be irrelevant or even (life) threatening. Due to different symptoms, incorrect dosages or different modes of action of medication, women receive poorer medical care. There is therefore a close connection between sexualized violence and structural discrimination, such as the gender pay gap, unequal career opportunities and gender data gaps in medicine, research and safety. It is therefore vital, in the truest sense of the word, to eliminate these injustices.
We read: sexualized violence is not always obvious or noticed by third parties. Nevertheless, it has a destructive effect - both personally and socially as well as in business. It often occurs quietly, almost unnoticed in everyday life. It is often trivialized and presented as normality, wrapped up in jokes, compliments or touching. Sexualized violence in the workplace is therefore an issue that we frequently encounter in our everyday working lives, but which we often do not consciously notice or recognize. This is partly due to the fact that perception depends on different interpretations - those of the perpetrators, the witnesses and the victims. Because everyone has their own experiences and experiences that make us so wonderfully unique. And lead to different perceptions and interpretations.

Perhaps you remember a situation in which you felt uncomfortable or witnessed a boundary violation that made you feel uncomfortable as a witness?

In such moments, it is important not to trivialize the experience. It is crucial to acknowledge that it is sexualized violence. In order to understand sexualized violence correctly, we must be aware that perceptions depend on the interpretation of words, gestures, actions and images. However, the decisive factor is how the victims experience and feel about the situation - their perspective must be taken seriously and sensitively.

Sexualized violence can have serious consequences for those affected, including mental and physical health problems, professional disadvantages, job loss, financial burdens and an impaired quality of life. These effects not only affect individuals, but also companies. They can be confronted with problems such as wasted resources, blocked potential and a possible standstill or regression.

Are you not yet convinced that sexualized violence in the workplace is an issue we need to talk about?

Are you familiar with inappropriate questions, for example in job interviews, in small talk or at company parties? Questions in which you were asked about your personal background, your sexuality or your relationship experiences? Even though these questions are not legally permitted?

"And where are your children when you're at work?"

"Why don't you smile, then I'll like you better."

"Tell me something about your relationship - how are things with your wife?"

Such questions are inappropriate, offensive and violate applicable discrimination laws[21]. They impair the chance of a fair interview in application situations. They cause talented people to turn down offered positions. They cause those affected to avoid events and thus become socially marginalized. They lead to tension and conflict in the workplace. They create a toxic work environment.

And often such questions can not only lead to these problems, they do!

Inappropriate questions, lewd comments, unwanted advances and sexist jokes are not uncommon, even among managers.

"I like it when you kneel in front of me."

"Well, are you asleep?"

"Blonde and stupid."

Bosses put pressure on employees by promising professional benefits for sexual favors or threatening to harm their careers if they refuse. They may take retaliatory measures or send suggestive messages with requests for sexual acts if inappropriate invitations are declined. Then it can happen that those affected supposedly voluntarily agree to a sexual act or further private conversations and meetings out of fear or to avoid negative consequences and to secure their own existence. However, this consent is given under considerable pressure and massive manipulation, meaning that the victim's decision is ultimately not voluntary. Perpetrators use their position of power to put the victim in a predicament, which makes this form of coercion to consent another facet of sexualized violence.

But manipulation is not the way to go!

And sexualized violence is unfortunately not an isolated case among colleagues either. Degrading and disrespectful statements are not uncommon. They contribute to the normalization of a toxic work culture. The problem is therefore not only limited to power relations in the hierarchy, but also exists on an equal level in order to maintain one's own power and weaken the power of others. Perhaps you are familiar with situations similar to this:

> A team of colleagues sits together in the canteen during the lunch break.
> Colleague A: "Do you know why women always go to the toilet in pairs?"
> Colleague B: "No, why?"
> Colleague A: "Because they can't cope with a decision on their own!"
> Colleague B and colleague C laugh, while colleague D, the only woman in the group, feels uncomfortable and suppresses her indignation.

Such comments should therefore not go unnoticed and uncommented on.

Perhaps colleague D laughs along in another situation because she finds the comment or the colleague funny. In this case, her personal perception is not affected. But what happens when other colleagues hear or hear about it? They too can feel hurt or devalued by such statements, even if the colleague present does not show or feel this.

The context and perception of such comments may vary, but the potential to cause harm remains. This is because spreading such images of women, as colleague A does, also affects all women, even if they are not present. Companies often have codes of conduct and policies to promote equality and respect in the workplace. Such comments may violate these policies and jeopardize the working environment, the well-being of the workforce, reputation and compliance with applicable law.

It is therefore not only the external perception of the people who were present in the situation that applies. Because shown and felt perceptions can vary. And the perception of other people is also crucial in a large team, such as in a company. This is where a great deal of tension arises, laden with misunderstandings, conflicts, risks and also opportunities. In order to reconcile this tension, we take a look behind the scenes at the different perceptions.

TRUE OR FALSE:
THE DILEMMA WITH PERCEPTIONS

For the understanding of subjective (personal) and objective (impartial and value-free) perception of incidents, there is no right or wrong interpretation.

There are inappropriate behaviors, sexual assaults, and other forms of sexualized violence. These always represent wrong behavior. However, when responding to such acts, there are a variety of differences. These differences should not be judged. They should be approached as neutrally as possible. Because each person experiences and interprets situations differently. What may seem like a harmless joke to one person can be deeply hurtful or degrading to another. There are, especially in companies, established guidelines that regulate the handling of such situations and aim to avoid them from the outset. They set out the desired behavior, what is not allowed, and how the culture in a company should be lived and strengthened.

In many cases, power relations and hierarchies are decisive in the perception of incidents. A person in a position of power may be less aware of how their comments or actions affect others, while the affected person may not dare to express their outrage or discomfort. Cultural and social norms also influence what is seen as acceptable or unacceptable. This leads to different expectations and perceptions of appropriate behavior. Gender-specific differences also play a significant role. Men and women sometimes have different experiences and perspectives when it comes to sexualized violence. What men may perceive as harmless, women may find threatening or offensive, and vice versa. The emotional reaction to incidents of sexualized violence varies widely. Some people may process such incidents quickly, while others may suffer profound psychological effects, such as anxiety, depression, or post-traumatic stress disorder. This variability in emotional response adds to the complexity. Legal and organizational frameworks also play a role. Different countries and companies have different laws and guidelines that define what constitutes sexualized violence and how to handle it.

The difficulties arising from differing perceptions are influenced by individual, social, cultural, and organizational factors. This diversity of perspectives and reactions often leads people to either make judgments to create order or ignore the problem because they are overwhelmed by addressing it. Therefore, clear and consistent solutions are needed that require a sensitive and nuanced approach to handling such incidents. Because: Sexualized violence affects people everywhere - in offices, in healthcare, in retail, in services, in government, in volunteer institutions, in the maritime industry, in industry, in trades, in construction, in schools, in aviation, in universities, in agriculture, and everywhere people meet and work together. There, we can be unintentionally touched, disadvantaged, pressured, sexualized, subjected to suggestive comments, objectified, and devalued.

Not nice, is it?

As authors, we have gathered many examples for this book from our own experiences and were shocked by the number of cases we have already encountered. It is alarming how frequently such situations occur and how urgently measures are needed to counteract them.

Both employers and employees need to be sensitized and actively work to prevent such incidents. It is high time to tackle these challenges head on and develop effective solutions. And if you are still not convinced, we will convince you with the hard facts - completely unemotional, clarified and scientifically tested.

CHAPTER 2

FACT CHECK
A LOOK AT STATISTICS AND RESEARCH

To better understand the extent of sexualized violence in the workplace, numerous studies and surveys have been conducted in recent years.

These investigations show that sexualized violence in the workplace is widespread.

However, only the so-called clear statistics—that is, the known reported or filed cases—can be captured.
The dark figure, meaning undocumented and unknown cases, remains hidden even with these surveys.

According to the study "Dealing with Sexual Harassment at the Workplace" by the Federal Anti-Discrimination Agency from 2019[22], only 23% of those affected have officially filed a complaint, and only 1% have taken legal action. The reasons for this are manifold and will be discussed in detail in the following chapters. We should definitely keep this gap in mind as we look at the available statistics.

Moreover, many of the existing studies predominantly focus on women as those affected. Research on violence against men and, in particular, non-binary individuals is still limited.

It is urgently necessary to close these research gaps in order to also address these groups and develop comprehensive prevention and intervention strategies. The focus on all affected groups is increasingly being considered in ongoing studies, which contributes to a better and fairer capture of reality.

AN UNEMOTIONAL LOOK: CURRENT STUDIES

The consideration of facts and data is crucial to capture the reality of sexualized violence in the workplace.

Perhaps you have already experienced sexualized violence?

Then you are not alone. Every eight minutes, a person in Germany experiences sexualized violence[23].

But sexualized violence in the workplace is a serious and widespread problem not only in Germany, but throughout Europe. According to an EU-wide survey[24], around 33% of women in the EU have experienced physical, sexual or psychological violence in adulthood. It found that one in three women have been sexually harassed in the workplace. Younger women report a higher prevalence: two out of five women have already been victims of sexual harassment at work. Worldwide, data from the International Labor Organization (ILO)[25] shows that 22.8% of workers have experienced at least one form of violence or harassment at work during their working lives. Women are particularly frequently affected by sexual violence and harassment, accounting for 6.3% or 205 million women.

Who is affected?

In October 2019, the Federal Anti-Discrimination Agency presented the study "Dealing with Sexual Harassment in the Workplace."[26] The study found that one in eleven working individuals (9% of respondents) had experienced sexual harassment in the workplace in the past three years. Women were affected more often (13%) than men (5%). An analysis[27] of over

700 court rulings showed that almost all cases involved women as victims. Additionally, 90% of counseling inquiries to the Federal Anti-Discrimination Agency[28] came from women. In a survey conducted by the agency, 22% of respondents reported experiencing inappropriate sexual questions, and 19% reported unwanted physical advances. Among men surveyed, 7% stated that they had been sexually harassed at work. They primarily reported verbal harassment, such as inappropriate questions (19%) and unwanted physical advances (12%).

According to the study "Sexual Harassment in the Workplace" conducted by the Social Science Survey Center Duisburg on behalf of the Federal Anti-Discrimination Agency[29], women experience significantly more physical harassment than men. Men, on the other hand, are more frequently exposed to offensive emails or ambiguous comments.

A 2018 study conducted as part of the "Public Service Citizen Survey"[30] found that 30% of employees had experienced sexual harassment or sexist behavior in the workplace. Of those, 15% were directly affected, with women (26%) more frequently affected than men (6%). Employees under 30 years of age were more often affected (22%) than older employees (12–16%). Public sector employees under collective agreements were more frequently affected than civil servants or private sector employees (20% vs. 15%).

Another study[31] shows that trans* individuals experience discrimination and harassment at an above-average rate. 33% reported being physically or sexually assaulted or threatened in Germany. Homosexual and bisexual people are also highly affected: 22% of lesbian women, 21% of gay men, 17% of bisexual women, and 14% of bisexual men reported experiencing discrimination in the workplace due to their sexual identity in the past twelve months.

Additionally, numerous other studies from insurance companies, trade unions, agencies, universities, and other organizations exist. When all studies are combined, the data suggests that in Germany, approximately one in four to five women and one in twelve to fourteen men experience sexualized violence in the workplace over the course of their careers.

Who are the perpetrators?

The 2019 study[32] by the Federal Anti-Discrimination Agency, "Dealing with Sexual Harassment in the Workplace," found that 53% of harassment cases were committed by individuals who were not employed by the companies, such as customers, clients, or patients. In 43% of cases, harassment came from colleagues, and in 19% of cases, from supervisors or individuals in higher positions. The risk of experiencing sexualized violence exists across all professional fields. However, incidents are particularly prevalent in the healthcare and social sector (29%), the industrial sector (11%), trade (12%), transportation (6%), the water and energy supply sector, and education (each 10%). People who work directly with customers are most affected, especially in the service industry (13%). The problem is also significant in academic professions and leadership roles (each 10%).However, this does not mean that sexualized violence does not occur in industries not explicitly mentioned here. No sector is free from such incidents! It is essential to remain vigilant and take active measures against sexualized violence in all areas.

What acts were committed?

The study "Dealing with Sexual Harassment in the Workplace"[33] also documented different forms of violence. The affected individuals experienced the following sexualized, harassing, and unwanted actions:

62%

Comments

44 %

Jokes or suggestive looks/gestures/catcalling

28 %

Intimate or sexualized questions

26%

Touching, cornering, physical advances

23%

Pictures, texts, films, messages

22%

Invitations to dates

11%

Requests for sexual acts

5 %

Indecent exposure

4 %

Blackmail, coercion, or force to engage in sexual acts

A statistic from the German Federal Ministry for Family Affairs[34], Senior Citizens, Women, and Youth shows that 63% of the surveyed women and 49% of the surveyed men have experienced or witnessed sexualized violence, also in the workplace, during their lifetime. Among these individuals, 83% have been affected multiple times. A significant proportion of those affected had to endure several such incidents in the past three years: 29% of women and 38% of men reported experiencing two to three such situations. The situation is particularly severe for 6% of the affected women, who each reported over 30 instances of harassment.

But that is not all.

Only 17% of female employees in Germany who have experienced violence in the form of unwanted touching, and just 13% of those who have been forced into sexual acts, have reported these incidents, as revealed by the survey European Observatory on Sexism and Sexual Harassment at Work conducted by the Jean Jaurès Foundation and the European Foundation for Progressive Studies[35].

The survey further found that, across Europe, younger women are disproportionately affected by sexualized violence, regardless of the form it takes. 42% of women under the age of 30 have experienced at least one form of sexualized violence in the workplace, compared to 28% of women in their thirties, 24% of women in their forties, and 16% of women in their fifties. This increased vulnerability among younger women is undoubtedly due to a greater "susceptibility caused by a lack of experience and self-confidence in early adulthood" as well as the fact that they often work in more exposed positions, particularly in jobs involving direct public interaction or where they wear uniforms that accentuate their body shape, such as retail, hospitality, or catering. From the perspective of male perpetrators, they thus conform to stereotypes of being sexually attractive and sexually available.

Moreover, the survey also highlights a higher prevalence of sexualized violence among women who fit dominant body shape stereotypes, as measured by Body Mass Index (BMI = body weight in relation to height): Women with a below-average BMI (29%) are twice as likely to be affected as those with an above-average BMI (17%). Another completely absurd form of discrimination.

There are also significant territorial disparities in sexualized violence against employees. The proportion of affected individuals in the workplace is twice as high in urban centers (18%) compared to rural communities (9%) or remote towns (9%). This disparity between urban and rural areas is likely due to the anonymity of large cities, which facilitates inappropriate behavior, especially in service-oriented jobs with public interaction. Additionally, the demographic structure of urban populations plays a role, as particularly vulnerable groups are overrepresented in cities.

These facts are alarming and are not limited to specific industries.

Industry-specific studies are equally concerning. A study conducted by the Berufsgenossenschaft für Gesundheitsdienst und Wohlfahrtspflege (BGW)[36] in 2021 found that in Germany's nursing and healthcare sector, 63% of inpatient staff reported experiencing non-verbal sexualized violence—such as exposure or being shown pornographic images—at least once in the past twelve months. Verbal sexualized violence was experienced by 69% of employees, and 53% reported experiencing physical or other forms of sexualized violence at least once in the same period.

Such statistics represent only the tip of the iceberg. Many cases go unreported, let alone prosecuted. The actual prevalence is therefore very likely to be much higher. Furthermore, these issues are often underreported in Germany. Nevertheless, the numbers speak for themselves: Sexualized violence in the workplace is a widespread issue that can no longer be ignored. And it is not only widespread but also a serious and multifaceted problem that extends far beyond immediate and visible actions.

To fully understand this complex issue and develop effective prevention strategies, experts are investigating the underlying causes that contribute to its occurrence, such as:

1. Power Structures and Hierarchies
A key factor in the occurrence of sexualized violence in the workplace is the existing power structures and hierarchies. Many organizations have clear power dynamics that create opportunities for abuse. Individuals in higher positions have greater influence and control, placing them in a privileged position. This power can be abused to exploit others and commit assaults.

2. Workplace Culture and Environment
Workplace culture plays a crucial role in both the emergence and tolerance of sexualized violence. A culture that tolerates or even encourages sexist or discriminatory jokes, comments, or behaviors creates an environment where such actions are perceived as acceptable and normal. In organizations where clear guidelines are lacking and where behavioral codes are not consistently enforced, undesirable patterns of behavior become entrenched and institutionalized.

3. Gender Stereotypes and Social Norms

Deeply rooted gender stereotypes and social norms also contribute to the occurrence of sexualized violence. Traditional notions of masculinity and femininity influence how different genders are perceived and treated in the workplace. If men are seen as dominant and women as subordinate, it fosters both the emergence and acceptance of sexualized violence. Gender biases become embedded in values and behaviors, creating an environment where sexist actions are not taken seriously and thus tolerated.

4. Lack of Awareness and Education

Another crucial factor is the lack of awareness and education. There is often a shortage of informational resources that educate employees about their rights and provide them with the necessary tools to act. Without adequate education, employees are unable to recognize harassment, respond appropriately, or report incidents.

5. Insufficient Legal and Organizational Frameworks

Inadequate legal and organizational frameworks also contribute to the occurrence of sexualized violence. In too many organizations, clear policies and procedures for reporting and handling assaults are either absent or not effectively enforced. Even when legal regulations exist, they are often poorly implemented in practice. A lack of comprehensive support for those affected, as well as unclear or ineffective measures for preventing and sanctioning sexualized violence, perpetuate the problem.

6. Individual Behavior and Personalities

Finally, individual behaviors and personality traits play a role. Perpetrators of sexualized violence may have personal attitudes or psychological issues that facilitate such actions. Factors such as a lack of empathy, immaturity, or an increased need for control can contribute to sexualized violence. Examining and raising awareness of these individual factors helps to develop targeted preventive measures and overarching solutions.

The emergence of sexualized violence in the workplace is therefore the result of a complex interplay of various factors. Analyzing these underlying causes is essential to developing effective prevention strategies and creating a safer and more respectful work environment.

NUMBERS THAT SPEAK:
COSTS THAT ALARM

And for those who still need more reasons to stand against sexualized violence, let's look at the costs:

According to a study by the European Institute for Gender Equality (EIGE)[37], the costs of gender-based violence in the EU amount to €366 billion per year. In Germany alone, the societal costs of domestic and sexualized violence against women are estimated at €54 billion per year, which equals €148 million per day. These figures do not even include costs for male and non-binary victims.

In 2016, the WAVE[38] network added that an investment of just 10% of these costs (i.e., €45 per citizen per year) in violence prevention would significantly reduce the financial impact on national budgets. Yet, far too little is being done.

Estimates suggest that the global GDP could increase by around 15%[39] if women were able to participate in economic life on an equal footing and without structural sexualized violence.

Our own experience and calculations show that corporate costs average €130,000 per affected person due to sexualized violence in larger companies and corporations.

So, what can – no, what must – we do?

It was a sunny Monday morning when Jari, a talented young lawyer, set off for work. Energized, he entered the office. But as soon as he stepped in, he sensed an unpleasant tension in the air. A colleague he had been working with for some time had repeatedly made inappropriate comments and touched him in an unwelcome way. Jari felt uncomfortable and harassed, but the thought of speaking up filled him with fear. "A man, and a lawyer at that, being sexually harassed by a renowned prosecutor? Who would believe him? Maybe he had misinterpreted it or even provoked it? And whom could he turn to for support?" he wondered. Jari feared that reporting the incidents could jeopardize – or even end – his career. Thus began a vicious cycle of violence, shame, guilt, and further violence.

Examples like Jari's show that sexualized violence in the workplace is a widespread yet highly tabooed issue.

The impact on victims is severe and becomes even heavier when surrounded by silence. The consequences range from psychological distress such as anxiety, depression, and post-traumatic stress disorder to career setbacks, including job loss and diminished career prospects, and in the worst cases, even suicide.

The first step is therefore the de-tabooing of experiences of sexualized violence in the workplace.

It is important that victims are encouraged to openly share their experiences—whether with colleagues, supervisors,

internal or external trusted persons. Clear guidelines and procedures must be in place to report such incidents and take effective measures that ensure both the protection of victims and the accountability of perpetrators.
Unfortunately, experience shows that victims often remain silent out of fear of negative consequences. That is why it is essential to foster an open, supportive, and trusting workplace culture where everyone can speak about their experiences and seek help without fear of retaliation.

Prevention plays a key role. This includes a targeted analysis of the causes of sexualized violence in the workplace, professional evaluation of the findings, and the implementation of appropriate measures to prevent further incidents.
A comprehensive awareness of sexualized violence in all its forms, clear definitions of inappropriate behavior, and concrete action guidelines on how everyone can actively counteract such incidents are essential.

Equally important is the support of all.

SUPPORT:
GIVING AND RECEIVING

Sexualized violence affects people regardless of gender, position, or hierarchy level. Perpetrators can appear in various roles, whether as supervisors, employees, or external business partners. This diversity and unpredictability make it more difficult to recognize and address abuse and assaults—and thus ensure that everyone receives the support that the company is both legally and morally obligated to provide.

For a long time, men were solely assigned the role of perpetrators, particularly in cases of harm targeting a person's gender or gender identity. While perpetrators are more often male colleagues or supervisors, it is important to consider all sides. A one-sided perspective makes it harder to perceive men and non-binary people as potential victims of violence and abuse and women and non-binary people as perpetrators. However, public awareness has now developed that sexualized violence can affect all genders and can be committed by anyone.

Everyone is affected. Anyone can be a perpetrator. To anyone..

Against this background, it is advisable to respond to both obvious sexualized violence, more subtle boundary violations, and disturbing behavior - no matter who they come from.

To minimize the negative consequences of sexualized violence that has already occurred in the workplace and to protect the victims, it is essential that employers offer easily accessible and appropriate support. This includes:

1. Immediate support and safety
This includes safe spaces, accommodation, medical care,

and psychological first aid.

2. Confidential counseling and support

Victims must have access to confidential and professional counseling and support from trained specialists, such as psychologists, social workers, or lawyers. These professionals help them cope with the emotional, psychological, and legal challenges.

3. Awareness for witnesses

Witnesses need to be sensitized and encouraged to report incidents and also receive appropriate support.

4. Sensitive and supportive work environment

Only in a sensitive and supportive work environment can victims speak openly about their experiences without fear of stigmatization or retaliation. Such an environment is created through clear guidelines and functioning procedures for reporting, training for all employees, as well as holistic protection concepts and victim-centered measures.

5. Legal support

Access to legal support helps victims understand their rights and take potential legal action. This includes assistance in filing complaints, access to legal contacts, and support during internal and external proceedings.

6. Sustainable support

Since the effects of sexualized violence in the workplace are long-lasting and sustainable, it is essential that victims receive long-term and sustainable support. This includes professional therapy, support during reintegration, or career reorientation.

Individual support is as unique as the act of violence itself and should always be tailored to the individual needs and personal wishes of the people involved. And this is not just a Nice to Have, but a Must Have and in many countries, it is similarly regulated.

GENERAL EQUAL TREATMENT ACT: OBLIGATIONS AND RIGHTS[40]

The General Equal Treatment Act in Germany - as an example - prohibits "sexual harassment," particularly in professional contexts.

Paragraph § 2 Section 1 No. 1-4

"Sexual harassment" includes actions that violate the dignity of the affected individuals or create a hostile, degrading, or humiliating environment.

Paragraph § 12

The employer is obliged to take appropriate measures to prevent "sexual harassment" and protect the affected individuals. This includes implementing and consistently enforcing codes of conduct and clear guidelines, as well as raising awareness among employees and management. In the context of discrimination, employers have a specific duty of protection towards their employees. This means they must inform them about legal protection and take preventive measures to make the working environment safer (duty of prevention and information). Every complaint must be taken seriously - whether it comes from supervisors, colleagues, clients, or other business partners, or whether they are accused. In each case, it must be determined whether specific protective measures need to be taken to ensure that the discrimination does not occur again in the future (duty of action).

Paragraph § 13

Employers and companies must establish a department where employees can file complaints if they have been discriminated against or harassed at the workplace.

Paragraph § 14

Employees who are affected by "sexual harassment" have the right to protection and support. The law requires employers to provide corresponding complaint channels and ensure that affected individuals can assert their rights without fear of negative consequences.

Paragraph § 15

Individuals who experience "sexual harassment" at the workplace may be entitled to compensation or damages in certain cases. This includes, for example, reimbursement of medical or therapy costs incurred due to the "sexual harassment" (damages). Compensation in the form of pain and suffering damages may also be possible. Employers are liable for "sexual harassment" if it is committed by individuals who hold an employer role or have authority, such as supervisors, HR departments, executives, or board members. If "sexual harassment" is committed by colleagues, employers are liable if no protective measures were taken and repeated incidents occur.

Apprentices

Apprentices must be protected just like any other employees. If employers fail to meet their duty of protection, the trade supervision authority or the vocational chamber can be involved, depending on the company. In such a case, the company may lose its qualification to offer apprenticeships (cf. Section § 33 of the Vocational Training Act BBiG). This is especially true if the individuals responsible for the training are also the employers.

Freelancers

Freelancers in an employee-like relationship (so-called permanent freelancers) are protected just like all other employees. However, it does not offer comprehensive protection against "sexual harassment" for freelancers, independent contractors, or employees under fixed-term contracts during their contractual relationship. The protection only extends to freelance workers if, for example, a client conditions the assignment of a contract on sexual actions. However, freelancers are not defenseless. Civil and criminal laws that concern defamation and (sexual) coercion provide a legal framework. Freelancers in an employee-like relationship (so-called permanent freelancers) are protected just like all other employees.

LAST WAY OUT TERMINATION: EXECUTIVES AS PERPETRATORS

When sexual violence is perpetrated by a person in the executive board, management, or ownership of a company, the situation often becomes very complicated. Even when the allegations are clear, legal protection may be ineffective, as employers may ignore feedback or downplay the actions. Since leaders don't self-report, sanction, or discipline, affected individuals often feel powerless. In most cases, they don't dare to make a report or file a complaint. They feel isolated, overwhelmed, and at the mercy of the power structures within the company. The fear of negative consequences with colleagues leads to a situation where affected individuals find it harder to be heard or find allies. Who would stand up to the management, especially when they deny the accusations, trivialize them, or threaten with legal action?

In such cases, it is even more important that external bodies are involved, such as trade regulatory offices, professional associations, or the Federal Anti-Discrimination Agency. They can offer support and outline further steps for the affected person's individual situation. This allows the individual to receive guidance and objectivity from independent bodies. They know their concerns will be taken seriously and, if possible and desired, they can move forward with further steps together.

However, even with such assistance, most affected individuals eventually resign, as further cooperation is simply unbearable. They often do so even if it puts them in a financially and socially precarious position. Through their self-initiated resignation, they often lose their entitlement to unemployment benefits or other support, which may be available in the case of a dismissal without notice or a mutual termination agreement. Therefore, the resignation can be an act of self-protection, but it often results from despair and frequently ends in emotional and existential distress.

It is also possible that the management will dismiss the affected person under a pretext to avoid direct confrontation with the allegations and to escape legal or reputational consequences. In such cases, the dismissal is used as a strategic tool to avoid the conflict and obscure their own responsibility. This type of termination can bring additional legal and emotional burdens for the affected individuals. Proving the connection between the sexual violence and the dismissal is difficult and requires the financial and emotional resources of the affected person to pursue and sustain such a procedure.

After a resignation or dismissal by the employer, employees remain in the company who are aware of the act and the subsequent circumstances. These employees will be wary of getting into a similar situation. They will either endure the actions, try to avoid the perpetrators, or resign themselves. Either way, the working atmosphere will worsen, rumors will increase, and insecurity will rise. Thus, companies not only lose employees but also trust – both internally and externally.

And what does the perpetrator do?

Perpetrators who emerge from such a situation without serious consequences have no reason to change their behavior. They can and will continue to exhibit misconduct unchallenged, unpunished, and unchecked.
This also applies to perpetrators who, after one or more incidents become known, are "promoted away," meaning they are transferred and may even receive a promotion. This problematic practice is used when supervisors or organizations want to cover up incidents and/or avoid processing (for whatever reasons). The motive is to solve the problem by transferring the person, removing them from contact and sight. The misconduct is neither confronted nor sanctioned. Instead, the person is placed in a position with even more power. This increases the risk that they will continue or even escalate their miscon-

duct. The unsuspecting new colleagues are at the mercy of the actions, and the problem repeats itself.

Companies do themselves no favors with this approach. By ignoring and downplaying misconduct, the trust of the workforce in leadership and justice within the company is severely damaged. At the same time, the "promotion away" process signals to other employees that misconduct in the company has no serious consequences or is even rewarded. This can significantly increase the frequency and severity of such incidents within the company and lead to a toxic atmosphere. If sexual violence is tolerated or not adequately sanctioned through promotion, it may constitute a violation of the employer's duty of care under the General Equal Treatment Act in Germany. Establishing a clear and consistent approach to addressing misconduct and ensuring that everyone is treated equally and works in a safe environment is therefore also in the interest of companies.

And it's not just the practice of "promoting away" that prevents proper intervention and sanctioning. Even if the executive or management team consists of multiple individuals who are informed about an incident, it does not mean that they will recognize it and take action.

Why?
Perhaps because they are subject to some of the erroneous reactions outlined in the next chapter.

CHAPTER 3

MISCONCEPTIONS
CHALLENGES AND SOLUTIONS

Sexualized violence in the workplace occurs in all types of work environments. We encounter it every day—on land, at sea, and in the air.

Ideally, we should be familiar with the topic and know what is true and what is not.

Instead, there are numerous myths and misunderstandings that only make the problem worse.

THE TRUTH:
EXPOSE MYTHS AND PREJUDICES

Only by recognizing and debunking false assumptions can we develop a better understanding of the severity of the problem. We can then practice an appropriate response, offer support, and follow the principle:

Only Yes means Yes!

Let's take a look at some of the most common myths surrounding sexualized violence to dismantle prejudices and create arguments.

Myth I: Sexualized violence in the workplace is rare.

False!

> In fact, sexualized violence in the workplace is widespread and occurs in a variety of work environments: offices, factories, restaurants, retail shops, educational institutions, shipping, service industries, aviation, industry, craftsmanship, self-employment, healthcare, IT, construction, agriculture, entertainment, security services, logistics, social services, the arts and culture sector, public services, transportation, and more. Sexualized violence affects people of all genders and sexual orientations—whenever people work together.

Myth II: Victims of sexualized violence provoked the incident or wanted the violence.

This is a dangerous misconception!

It is never the victim's fault when they are subjected to sexualized violence in the workplace. The responsibility always lies with the perpetrator. It doesn't matter how the victim was dressed, how they behaved, or what their relationship with the perpetrator was. Everyone has the right to work in an environment free from sexualized violence.

Myth III: Victims report the incident immediately.

This is often not the case.

The barriers are often too high. Victims struggle greatly to report the incident—out of fear of negative consequences like retaliation, job loss, social isolation, or damage to their reputation. These concerns prevent a swift response and thus protect the perpetrators. Employers often don't perceive the action or the perpetrators as the problem but instead focus on the person reporting the incident. Psychological or emotional reasons also stop victims from talking about their experience. However, it is important to note: everyone has the right to choose the timing and manner of how they talk about sexualized violence and whether, how, and where the incident should be reported.

Myth IV: Sexualized violence in the workplace only involves physical abuse.

Definitely not!

Sexualized violence in the workplace can take various forms, including physical, verbal, non-verbal, or psychological violence. This includes "sexual harassment," unwanted touching, suggestive comments or jokes, inappropriate looks, discrimination based on gender or sexual orientation, and more. The term "sexualized violence" specifically includes any form of boundary violation and overstepping to counter this myth.

Myth V: Victims of sexualized violence can usually quickly overcome the incident.

No!

It is a widespread misconception that victims of sexualized violence can quickly process their experience once an incident is addressed. It is not "out of sight, out of mind." On the contrary, the impacts can be massive and existential—physically, emotionally, and psychologically—both in the short and long term. Additionally, it is not the responsibility of the victim to deal with the consequences of the violence alone. Support and professional help, such as therapy or legal advice, are necessary—even in the workplace.

Myth VI: Suggestive comments or jokes aren't that bad.

Another fairytale!

This is a serious misconception with harmful consequences. Sexualized violence, even in the form of suggestive comments, inappropriate sexual innuendos, or obscene jokes, is not harmless and remains a form of violence. It significantly harms the victim's well-being and violates their dignity. It is also unacceptable harassment.

Myth VII: Men cannot be affected by sexualized violence.

Der besonders weit verbreitete Irrtum!

Men are also affected by sexual harassment, sexual coercion, or discrimination based on their gender. Sexualized violence knows no gender boundaries and can affect anyone, regardless of gender or position within a company. Notably, men and male-presenting individuals within the LGBTQIA+ community are also heavily affected by sexualized violence.

Myth VIII: As long as the victim does not explicitly resist, it is not sexualized violence.

On the contrary!

Unwanted behavior, whether in the form of physical touch, sexual innuendos, or threats, should always be considered unwanted—objectively—regardless of whether it is explicitly rejected. It is not the victim's responsibility to legitimize or accept the behavior of the perpetrator. The myth that victims must clearly and explicitly resist in order for their experiences to be taken seriously only leads to shame, guilt, and blame. Sexualized violence is never acceptable, regardless of the victim's reaction or behavior. Such behavior should not be up for discussion, but regarded as unacceptable and treated accordingly.

Myth IX: Someone will intervene if sexualized violence occurs.

A deceptive and convenient assumption!

Instead, victims are often met with ignorance, denial, and indifference. Fears of one's own involvement often prevent bystanders from intervening. Furthermore, they rarely offer the necessary support or address the problem comprehensively. There is often a lack of understanding and protection plans, a lack of confidence in victim-appropriate behavior, and the absence of zero-tolerance cultures.

Myth X: The victim just wants attention!

Ha! Hahaha!

This statement trivializes the experiences that victims go through. This accusation ignores the reality of the violence experienced. It contributes to stigmatization and sows distrust towards those who have the courage to speak about their experiences. Studies and statistics show that false accusations are rare. The overwhelming majority of reports are based on real experiences. These must be recognized as such, even if it is uncomfortable and painful.

UNSUPPORTIVE ATTITUDES: VICTIM-BLAMING AND MORE

The consequences of false ideas and attitudes are far-reaching and have serious repercussions.

After a violent experience, victims are often confronted with victim-blaming (reversing the perpetrator-victim relationship), victim-bashing (insulting the victim), secondary victimization (being victimized further), and trivialization. These behaviors result in victims of violence and abuse being blamed for the wrongs they have suffered, which intensifies their suffering and hinders their recovery.

Victim-Blaming

"Why didn't you just say no?"

"With such a short dress, you provoked it yourself!"

"You're to blame! This sort of thing doesn't happen to me..."

Such statements imply that the affected person is responsible for the violence they experienced—due to how they dress, behave, or speak. This shifts the focus away from the perpetrators and contributes to demeaning the victims. This post-fact justification of the event by perpetrators, observers, or completely uninvolved people obscures the actual responsibility of the perpetrators. Instead, it demonstrates a lack of courage and understanding of the victim's situation. The perpetrator-victim reversal serves to deflect guilt or responsibility for the wrongdoing from the wrongdoer. However, such statements foster a culture that enables perpetrators to continue committing violence and expanding it.

Victim-Bashing

"She just wanted attention!"

"Why did he stay silent for so long?"

"She's lying!"

In victim-bashing, victims are defamed, insulted, humiliated, and belittled. This happens on social media, through public statements, or gossip. The victim is not only blamed for the injustice they suffered, but is often personally attacked, accused of lying, and their credibility is undermined. Such attacks significantly increase the victim's psychological burden and marginalize them. This creates cultures of silence and fear.

Secondary Victimization

"Come back tomorrow for the report, I'm done for the day!"

"In reality, you probably enjoyed it..."

"I don't believe you!"

A particularly insidious phenomenon is secondary victimization, also called "secondary traumatization" or "further victimization." It occurs when victims are hurt again after the initial act by the behavior of individuals, institutions, or society. While primary victimization refers to the direct harm caused by the act itself, secondary victimization refers to the intensification of the original trauma due to inappropriate reactions from the social environment and formal social control. The person is then doubly affected: by the act they experienced and the reactions of those around them. In this context, stereotypical judgments, myths, and beliefs in a just world—beliefs that crumble for the victim - also come into play. Necessary assistance is then not provided in a timely or adequate manner. Instead, sensational or improper claims, rumors, or media reports exacerbate the victim's trauma. This insufficient or insensitive treatment can occur from individuals or institutions like the police, judiciary, or healthcare systems. One example is a victim being aggressively interrogated in court, with their credibility questioned - an unmistakable case of secondary victimization.

Trivialization

"He's such a nice guy, he would never do that."

"It didn't look like she felt uncomfortable!"

"You always have to exaggerate..."

Trivialization downplays the seriousness or significance of an incident—by using euphemistic language, denying facts, or minimizing the impact. Such trivializations occur individually, in media, political statements, or in public discourse, for example, by:

The use of euphemisms
Instead of talking about "sexualized violence," terms like "inappropriate behavior" reduce the seriousness of the

incident.

Minimization
When a situation is described as a "small argument" or a "harmless joke," the real extent of the problem is not taken seriously or laid out.

Denial or ignoring of facts
Whenever something "can't be" or "must have been different," or when someone says, "we don't have that here," facts are ignored, realities are distorted, and obvious problems are neither acknowledged nor recognized. This blocks possible processing and solutions, silencing people.

Confirmation Bias

"Of course - als always..."

"Typical!"

"I would've noticed that!"

These are typical reactions of confirmation bias. Confirmation bias refers to a cognitive distortion where people selectively choose and interpret information to confirm their existing beliefs. Information that aligns with our worldview is noticed more than information that contradicts it or challenges our perspective. Confirmation bias also influences our perception of sexualized violence. People who, for example, believe that it mainly occurs in certain industries or is perpetrated by specific groups, tend to notice and give more weight to such reports, while ignoring or downplaying opposing information. This leads to underestimating the seriousness of such incidents, treating assaults as isolated cases, or placing them only in certain "problematic" industries. This bias contributes to trivialization and blocks necessary education and awareness. However, there are ways to counteract confirmation bias, such as using the:

Think the Opposite-Strategy

The "Think the Opposite" strategy involves consciously adopting the opposite perspective. In the context of sexualized violence at the workplace, this means asking: "What examples challenge role norms in my industry?" or "Are there industries where respectful behavior is promoted despite difficult conditions?" or "What examples do I know where people are treated equally regardless of their gender?" This method strengthens a more balanced perspective and mindset.

However, if people do not counteract these wrong reactions, the impact can be severe. They can lead to deep feelings of isolation, shame, and self-doubt in the victims, drastically reducing their willingness to seek help. So if these wrong reactions are so damaging, why do they occur at all?

Because they serve to maintain one's worldview, personal security, and normative values. They protect against the uncomfortable realization that a violent act could also happen to the person reacting wrongly or to others. Rather than confronting the actual realization of helplessness and accepting that actions happen independently of external circumstances, people try to gain emotional and psychological security by constructing a false sense of superiority and illusory control:

"It won't happen to me because I behave differently."

"I would have handled the situation!"

"I don't look like a victim..."

Such thoughts and statements give the person reacting wrongly a sense that they have control over life and its risks, maintain or restore social harmony. They want to avoid the admission of the full extent of the wrongdoings because it could lead to social tensions, personal consequences, personal recognition of their mistakes, or even the need for behavioral and attitudinal change. These wrong reactions are supported by socially constructed gender roles or behaviors, which can be used as convenient explanations for why the act "was deserved" or "could have been avoided":

"A respectable woman doesn't behave like that!"

"If he had been more confident, it wouldn't have happened."

"Anyone who works in that job should expect this."

This self-deception or overestimation serves to protect the ego, calm oneself, deny one's own vulnerability, and avoid the need for showing empathy. These behaviors do not foster exchange or solutions. On the contrary! They contribute to perpetrators remaining unpunished, and victims not receiving appropriate support and justice.And worse yet: Defending victims are often portrayed as oversensitive, whiny, hysterical, or quarrelsome—by perpetrators, superiors, fellow victims, witnesses, uninvolved persons, and even contact persons.

Who is hysterical?

These attributions don't help. They demean the experiences and emotions of the victims, undermine their credibility, and lay the foundation for further offenses. Victims who decide to report an incident, but are not taken seriously by colleagues or superiors, even mocked, will not turn to these people or anyone else in the future. Incidents will then not be investigated, and perpetrators can continue their actions unimpeded. Perhaps the next incident will affect people who reacted wrongly earlier. Their perspective will suddenly and drastically change.

To avoid such perspective shifts generated by incidents, we should address this in advance. We achieve this by breaking down false ideas and attitudes and creating awareness that sexualized violence in the workplace is never acceptable. Victims must be treated with respect, without blame, and instead be supported with sensitivity to their experiences.

THE PINK-BLUE TRAP: NOT JUST FOR CHILDREN

The "Pink-Blue Trap" describes the norm of pushing people into specific roles and behaviors based on their gender, often rooted in traditional gender roles. This phenomenon appears in various aspects and influences how we see, evaluate, and treat people. The term "Pink-Blue Trap" originates from the practice of distinguishing and treating newborns based on gender: girls are often dressed in pink clothes and accessories, while boys are equipped with light blue items.

This color coding is more than just an aesthetic choice: it is part of a broader system of biases and norms that tie specific expectations to behavior, interests, and roles. In practice, this means:

For Girls

Pink, in all its shades, is traditionally associated with qualities such as gentleness, care, grace, charm, and emotionality. This color symbolism is also reflected in societal expectations and role patterns, particularly affecting girls. In many cultures, pink is considered a typical girl's color, which subtly suggests that girls should be interested in social and caregiving roles, styling and fashion, or nurturing work. This is linked to a larger social construct that normatively defines gender-specific roles and interests, often reinforcing these roles unconsciously through cultural symbols like colors. From a psychological perspective, associating the color pink with qualities like gentleness and caring can have profound effects on the development of gender identity and self-perception. When girls are subtly pushed into certain role models by societal signals, this can influence their interests, ambitions, and self-concepts. The connotation of pink as a female color may lead girls to follow this attribution and choose careers and activities considered typically feminine, potentially preventing them from engaging in traditionally male-associated areas such as STEM fields (Science, Technology, Engineering, and Mathematics). This can result in the reinforcement of gender stereotypes and a gender-specific separation in education and careers. At the same time, the limitation of color choices and the associated stereotyping can cause girls to suppress their own abilities and interests in order to conform to expected social norms.

For Boys

Light blue and other shades of blue are often associated with strength, concentration, independence, confidence, clarity, and rationality. These color associations have deep-rooted cultural and psychological dimensions. Psychologically, shades of blue promote feelings of calmness and trust and are often seen as conducive to concentration and analytical thinking. This explains why these colors are commonly used in contexts related to logic, objectivity, and decision-making. In social and cultural upbringing, boys are traditionally encouraged to be interested in technology, sports, logic, and leadership roles. This encouragement is often part of a larger system of gender roles and expectations, urging boys to develop qualities such as independence and assertiveness. The colors blue and light blue are thus not just aesthetic preferences but also symbols for certain personality traits and professional inclinations. However, these cultural norms and color codings, just like with girls, can inhibit or restrict the development of individual interests and talents.

These norms are deeply ingrained in our culture. Take a look at toy stores, advertising, children's accessories, children's care products, or clothing stores. These color allocations are still made today—even for adult items. Despite increasing protests from consumers, to which manufacturers, distributors, and brands must respond, stereotypical color assignments and expectations continue. These influence not only the development and behavior of children but also shape the behavior of adults well into old age. This highlights the importance of conscious upbringing, which allows everyone to develop and express their individual talents and inclinations beyond color symbolism and gender stereotypes. A mindful approach to these traditional ideas helps to question roles and foster a broader range of opportunities for all. After all, such color assignments, like pink for girls and (light) blue for boys, begin in infancy and continue throughout life. These stereotypes manifest in various areas of life and contribute to gender socialization. They influence which toys are offered to children, what professions they consider suitable, and how they develop their self-image. In advertising and media, these color assignments are often reinforced, further cementing perceptions of gender roles. Products for women are then presented in pastel tones, while products for men appear in bolder colors, (unconsciously) signaling which items are for which gender.

For example, the bath additive "Surprise Dino" in greenish-blue with powerful dinosaur images sits next to the bath additive "Galupy Mermaid" in pink-lavender glitter design with cute-looking mermaid unicorns.
Why not pink dinosaurs and blue unicorns? Or both in orange? Since there are no mermaids or unicorns, and the actual appearance of dinosaurs in terms of color and scales or feathers is not definitively determined, there are clearly many more combinations to choose from. How often are footballs

advertised with boys playing football? And beside them, craft kits for girls? Predictable and boring. At least with the above products, the classification often no longer mentions "girls" or "boys," but only "children." A gradual change has been occurring here for several years. Very slowly and cautiously, but:

At least it's a start.

To accelerate this change, not only manufacturers but also purchasing departments and we as consumers are called upon. Why not shop independently? Men look fantastic in pink shirts. Women look great in blue shoes. Girls can play football, and boys can dance ballet. We can all do anything.

Therefore, companies are well-advised to say goodbye to stereotypes and offer a much more diverse and broadly developed range. Because the Pink-Blue Trap, combined with many other role attributions and norms, has far-reaching effects:

Limited Opportunities
Rigid gender roles limit both professional and personal opportunities, particularly when role models are missing who embody alternative models. When certain groups or genders are rarely or never represented in particular professions or life areas, it becomes harder for others to take these paths. The gap in role model representation reinforces the perception that certain roles or professions are gender-specific and leads people to engage in more restricted opportunities, abandon certain career paths, or face rejection and degradation.

Professional Discrimination
Adults who do not conform to traditional gender roles

often face prejudice and discrimination. Women in leadership positions or men in caregiving professions deviate from expectations and often face additional challenges. This deviation is often accompanied by biases and normative assumptions that hinder professional recognition and personal development. Think about male flight attendants. How often are they labeled as "gay stewardesses" and hear such comments? And all because their job does not fit the traditional image of masculinity and is more associated with the "sexy stewardess." This image is also deeply sexist. The reality is that flight attendants are highly qualified and committed professionals, regardless of gender or the societal prejudices they have to overcome.

Self-Perception and Identity
Prejudices regarding gender also influence how people see themselves and develop their identity. This can lead to insecurities and a lack of self-confidence when someone does not meet the prescribed role models. One's confidence in abilities and potential diminishes when society doesn't expect it from them. This often leads people to give up their career goals and personal ambitions or not pursue them at all because they neither conform to the expectations nor want to break away from them. As a result, potential remains untapped, and boundaries emerge for personal and professional development.

Social Expectations and Interactions
Expectations of male and female behavior also affect how people are perceived and treated in social interactions. For example, men who seek emotional support or show care may be considered less masculine, while women who show leadership qualities may be seen as unfeminine. Since stereotypically female behavior is often

associated with low status and domesticity, it can be advantageous for women to demonstrate stereotypical masculine behaviors at work. In this way, they can show that they "have what it takes" to succeed. However, women who are attributed a claim to power often face significant sanctions. For instance, women who exhibit male-dominated behaviors are less likely to be hired, even if they are considered competent. This leads to the paradoxical situation where women avoid stereotypically feminine behavior to be perceived as knowledgeable, yet face resistance because they violate gender norms. These ideas thus result in people being treated differently in social and professional contexts than their actual abilities and qualifications would suggest. Men often abandon jobs dominated by women[41] due to societal stigmatization, with some even preferring unemployment over such a position. Some people conform to societal expectations and norms to meet these demands, while others consciously defy these norms to forge new paths or cross societal boundaries. This process of adapting to or breaking with social expectations holds both opportunities and challenges and contributes to the ongoing negotiation of gender roles and identities.

There are many other social or developmental psychological factors that influence the formation and development of gender roles. Developmentally, studies show that children already understand gender roles at preschool age and often adopt them uncritically. Such early experiences and the observation of gender-specific behavior in their environment contribute to the formation and reinforcement of stereotypes. Therefore, these factors should be recognized and consciously changed in a modern society that advocates for equality and diversity.

COGNITIVE DISSONANCE: WHEN WE THINK DIFFERENTLY THAN WE ACT

One way to better understand the dynamics of sexualized violence is to engage with cognitive dissonance. This describes the psychological state in which a person is confronted with conflicting thoughts, beliefs, or values. This conflict is often resolved by adjusting or justifying thoughts or actions. In the context of sexualized violence, cognitive dissonance manifests in various ways, both for perpetrators, victims, and bystanders.

Perpetrators Who Think Differently Than They Act

For perpetrators, cognitive dissonance arises when their actions do not align with their own moral values. For example, someone who sees themselves as kind and respectful will experience significant inner conflict when they realize their behavior was sexist or aggressive. To reduce this internal tension, perpetrators rationalize their actions, shift the blame onto the victim, or believe the victim deserved the act.

> *A supervisor who considers herself feminist but makes misogynistic comments reduces this dissonance by claiming her remarks were harmless or "perhaps a bit too direct," or that the victim "can't handle criticism." This way, she tries to reduce the discrepancy between her self-image and her behavior.*

This self-justification helps her maintain the image of being a reasonable person while not fully or at all acknowledging her mistakes.

Victims Who Think Differently Than They Act

Victims of sexualized violence also experience cognitive dissonance. They are often caught in an inner conflict between their self-image as a valuable and respected person and what has happened to them. This discrepancy leads to self-doubt and feelings of guilt.

> A person who has been harassed may think, "I just didn't behave properly..." or "It wasn't that bad, I shouldn't make such a drama out of it..." These thoughts serve as a coping mechanism to reduce cognitive dissonance.

By downplaying the experience or blaming themselves, the victim may make the inner conflict and emotional stress associated with the experience seem more bearable. However, this process complicates the healing journey and causes the victim to feel even more isolated and insecure.

Bystanders Who Think Differently Than They Act

Bystanders and employees who are aware of the act also experience cognitive dissonance when their observations or experiences contradict their values, beliefs, or expectations. When someone believes in fundamental values like justice and fairness, it can be extremely difficult to confront the fact that such values are being violated in their own environment, perhaps even by trusted team members. For example, if someone hears a sexist remark, they might try to downplay what they've heard:

"It was just a one-time slip-up."

"It wasn't that bad."

"Only a few people heard it..."

his helps align their perception with reality and protects them from the stress of realizing something is wrong in their environment. Dissonance also occurs when bystanders are unsure how to respond. They may face a decision of whether to confront, report, or ignore the behavior. The fear of possible consequences, like disrupting the work environment or receiving negative reactions from colleagues, leads to internal conflict. In this uncertainty, passive or ineffective decisions are made to avoid the contradiction—and often result in even more dissonance. For the tension between the desire to act correctly and actual inaction or indecision leads to emotional stress.
To support all those directly or indirectly involved and break personal and structural patterns, it is essential to develop awareness of these psychological mechanisms. For perpetrators, this means acknowledging their mistakes and not protecting them through self-justification. For victims, it is crucial to find support in clarifying their perception of what happened and in feeling valued and respected. For companies, it is important to improve structural conditions that enable sexualized violence.

Companies Who Present Themselves Differently Than They Act

Dissonance can also be visible in business contexts. This happens when companies advocate for values and present themselves in a way that contradicts how they actually act.

A company publicly and prominently advocates for equality. The management regularly emphasizes the values of equality, meaning equal opportunities for all. Nevertheless, reports repeatedly surface about sexist comments, harassment, and favoritism towards certain employees within the company, particularly from leadership or influential team members. The company earns the label "gender-washing" from employees and external parties.

This dissonance in the business context manifests in:

Public Engagement vs. Actual Behavior
The company faces a conflict between its public stance and the actual conditions in the workplace. While it presents itself as a model of respect and fairness to the outside world, the internal working conditions and behavior within the company do not align with the values it promotes. This leads to a contradiction that undermines trust in the leadership and damages the company's image.

Response to Complaints
Rather than seriously investigating reports of harassment and taking comprehensive actions to address the issues, leaders attempt to minimize or reframe the situation. They portray reports as isolated incidents or downplay the accusations. The company follows this interpretation instead of addressing the underlying problems, further increasing the dissonance between public statements and actual actions.

Internal Measures
To reduce dissonance, the company takes superficial

measures, such as publishing harassment policies or conducting general training. However, these measures are insufficient to bring about profound structural changes. No substantial adjustments to company policies or the code of conduct are made. The measures serve only to maintain the outward appearance of engagement without substantial changes in handling complaints or behavior.

Handling Feedback
Employees and outsiders experience that their complaints are either not taken seriously or not adequately addressed. No effective steps are taken to change problematic behaviors or to actually uphold the company's stated values and standards. This leads to the feeling that their concerns are being ignored or mishandled, further contributing to the discrepancy between the company's values and lived reality.

The company attempts to maintain the image of being a model and respectful organization, while the reality of the work environment contradicts the publicly stated values. This contradiction is only resolved by the following actions:

Transparent and Honest Communication
Press releases, internal publications, newsletters, emails, and information on the company website and social media regularly update on existing issues and the steps being taken to resolve them. Communication channels openly and honestly report on progress and challenges. Furthermore, employees and business partners are invited to share their own experiences, insights, and ideas to foster continuous dialogue and strengthen trust in leadership and the brand.

Active Involvement

All employees and management are actively involved in the change process. This means integrating their experiences and perspectives into company policy to ensure that the measures taken genuinely meet the needs and expectations of all parties. This can be done through feedback rounds, workshops, and joint decision-making processes. While involving everyone can be time-consuming, it contributes to the sustainable development of relevant measures, strengthens engagement, and increases acceptance of the changes.

Taking Comprehensive Action

Based on the involvement of all stakeholders and the analysis of surveys and feedback, a practical and implementable catalog of measures is created. This catalog is clearly defined and consistently implemented. It includes concrete improvements in the work environment, such as specialized training, changes in company policies, new behavioral standards, and certifications. Regular reviews and adjustments ensure that the measures remain effective and are adapted to current challenges.

Through these comprehensive steps, the contradiction between the public image and reality is addressed and overcome in the long term. In this way, the company's values are not only communicated externally but are also firmly embedded internally. This leads to increased credibility, improved reputation, and a stronger overall attractiveness of the company.

A holistic strategy that combines individual and structural action provides effective support and sustainable positive change in harmony.

STABLE VALUES:
THINKING AND ACTING IN HARMONY

A person believes that gender equality is important and that gender stereotypes should be overcome. Yet, when choosing gifts for children, they fall into the pink-blue trap. This leads to cognitive dissonance, as their behavior (purchasing gender-colored products) does not align with their belief (gender equality and rejection of stereotypes). This contradiction may also manifest physically in the form of discomfort or a sense of inconsistency.

Similar to a discordant note disrupting a harmonious melody, this is what it feels like when the inner imbalance becomes perceptible or visible, created when our beliefs and actions are not in harmony. However, we humans strive for harmony and need conflict-free environments to feel comfortable and act without disturbance. Therefore, we need a strategy to deal with cognitive dissonance. Change strategies, in this case, include:

Behavioral Change

The person can actively address this contradiction and consciously decide to choose colors in the future that they personally like, are considered gender-neutral, or consciously break with stereotypes. This way, they better reflect on their beliefs and reduce inner dissonance.

Openness to Beliefs

The person can consciously become open to the idea that, in certain situations, it is acceptable to consider individual preferences, even if they align with traditional gender roles.

It is not about protesting by only buying other colors or rejecting these colors. It is more about making flexible and reflective decisions that are adapted to the situation at hand. And doing so without unconsciously promoting prejudices and traditional norms. Through conscious choices, dissonances are reduced or dissolved, leading to a more unified and coherent self-image, where beliefs and values are in harmony.
To cope with cognitive dissonance, one must actively engage with prejudices and behavioral patterns. This is often uncomfortable but necessary in order to act authentically. It requires awareness of one's thoughts and actions as well as the courage to question oneself critically and openly and allow for change. This is a crucial step in shedding old behaviors and adopting an attitude that truly opposes all forms of sexualized violence.

Cognitive dissonance concerning sexualized violence can be changed not only on a personal level but also on a societal and workplace level through:

Education and Awareness
Awareness campaigns and educational programs that address sexualized violence and question societal norms and stereotypes increase the perceived dissonance between our beliefs and what we experience or observe. This pushes us to rethink and adjust our behaviors.

Public Discussions and Media Coverage
By promoting open discussions in the workplace, in the media, and in public, the taboo surrounding sexualized violence is broken. Personal testimonies, documentaries, social media posts, academic studies, campaigns,

exhibitions, films, podcasts, research, and discussions in networks all help raise awareness. Initially, this increases cognitive dissonance but, in the long run, leads to a stronger motivation to advocate against sexualized violence and align our behaviors with personal beliefs.

Promotion of Support Systems
Visible support networks foster societal pressure and underscore the seriousness of the issue. This highlights the contradiction between the knowledge of sexualized violence's existence and the actual response to it, leading to greater societal engagement.

Changing Norms and Values
Changing societal norms and values takes time. For this, age-appropriate and holistic awareness starting in early childhood is important and necessary. The issue of sexualized violence should also be present in schools, vocational training, higher education, and the workplace. The change of norms and values concerning sexualized violence is a continuous and multi-layered process. Education and awareness are the key to questioning deeply rooted societal beliefs and encouraging us to reflect on our own behaviors.

CHAPTER 4

PAINFUL REALITY
CONSEQUENCES FOR ALL

Sexualized violence in the workplace often has serious consequences for the affected employees and all those involved.

The consequences range from psychological and physical strain to social and existential impacts. Understanding these consequences leads to the realization of the importance of prevention, intervention, and support.

Because the consequences of sexualized violence are felt both directly and long-term.

VISIBLE AND INVISIBLE SCARS:
PHYSICAL, PSYCHOLOGICAL AND SOCIAL

Since coping strategies and impacts vary individually, we need a comprehensive understanding of the specific effects on each person involved in order to implement tailored measures. For this, we must know the possible consequences.

Impact on Victims

Many studies and statistics highlight the importance of prevention and support for victims by illustrating the serious consequences of sexualized violence in the workplace. In the aforementioned study by the Federal Ministry for Family Affairs, Senior Citizens, Women and Youth, 42% of affected women and 28% of affected men reported feeling humiliated and degraded to a moderate or very strong degree due to the actions they experienced. Moderate to very strong psychological distress was experienced by 41% of affected women and 27% of affected men. 30% of women and 21% of men also perceived the situation as moderately to highly threatening.

More than half of those affected by sexualized violence at the workplace suffer from psychological distress. Physical health problems, such as sexually transmitted infections and injuries, also occur in those affected by physical sexualized violence at work. Studies have shown that victims are at increased risk of developing post-traumatic stress disorder (PTSD), leading to long-term emotional and social challenges. Victims often feel guilty, even though they are never responsible for what has been done to them and what they had to endure. Nonetheless, they are ashamed of the situation they found themselves in and still find themselves in. They often hesitate to accuse anyone of misconduct. They feel isolated and are concerned about experiencing difficulties in relationships, work, or social interactions. Some withdraw from their social circles, avoiding contact with others—out of fear or shame to avoid stigmatization and misunderstanding. Some victims suppress their experiences of sexualized violence, which then often manifest in anxiety disorders, depression, or addiction. Often, victims direct their perceived anger towards themselves and engage in self-harm. In some cases, suicide attempts or completed suicides occur.

Impact on Witnesses

The impact of sexualized violence in the workplace is not limited to the directly affected employees but extends to those who have witnessed or heard about the violent acts. They can also be traumatized and suffer from the consequences. They feel guilt or fear, especially if they were unable to prevent or intervene in the violence. The emotional burden is severe, and dealing with it is difficult. The possible psychological effects are diverse: PTSD, anxiety, or depression are among them. Memories of the violent act burden them and trigger feelings of guilt, especially if they feel they didn't do enough to stop the violence or support the affected person. Additionally, they face social impacts. They have difficulty talking to others about their experiences or withdraw to avoid distressing memories and cognitive dissonances.

Impact on Perpetrators

Sexualized violence in the workplace affects not only the victims and witnesses but also the perpetrators. While they bear the responsibility, the impact on them should not be overlooked in order to gain a comprehensive picture. Perpetrators suffer from various consequences that their behavior brings. These include feelings of guilt, fear of legal consequences, loss of professional and social reputation, and significant emotional strain.

It is still important to emphasize that perpetrators are responsible for their behavior and legal consequences are appropriate! Involving the perpetrators does not mean that they are shielded from consequences or that their responsibility is reduced. However, a sustainable change is needed that also holds perpetrators accountable. Their participation is an essential part of solutions through awareness, responsibility, and behavioral change.

IN THE SHADOW OF FEAR:
THE FEAR OF STIGMATIZATION

"Don't be so dramatic!"

"It happened so long ago."

"Have you tried exercising?"

Such statements are not only inappropriate, but they also don't help. Instead, they further discriminate. They diminish the experiences and feelings of the listener, trivialize actions, and add to the burden. Rather than ignoring the issue or brushing it off quickly, it is important to approach those affected with empathy, support, and respect, and to honor their experiences and needs.

Don't be so dramatic!

This statement expresses a dismissive attitude and implies that the affected person is overreacting or complaining unnecessarily. As a result, the person feels not taken seriously, isolated, and suppresses their feelings.

It happened so long ago.

This statement suggests that the time passed since the incident should have diminished the feelings or consequences for the affected person. This frustrates those affected and gives them the impression that their experiences are unimportant or inconvenient and should be forgotten as soon as possible.

Have you tried exercising?

This statement implies that physical activity alone is enough to deal with the effects of sexualized violence. It ignores the complexity of traumatic experiences and their impact on the psychological and emotional health of the individuals involved. Instead of offering hasty and unconsidered advice, empathy and professional support are required.

Unfortunately, people often hear such statements.
It is understandable, therefore, that they hesitate to expose themselves to additional emotional and social burdens. The fear of additional hardships is immense:

Fear of...
... social exclusion.
... existential consequences.
... prejudice and accusations.
... trauma triggers.
... stigmatization and feelings of shame.
... loss of self-determination.
... mistrust.
... loss of trust.
... psychological and physical consequences.
... loss of relationships.
... refusal of help.
... concern.

Yes, it is a hard struggle to cope with the effects of sexualized violence at the workplace.

Sensitivity, openness, and dignity in our interactions are essential. Those affected need support through professional therapy, counseling, medical care, and help from loved ones. Employers are responsible for providing appropriate support systems, such as reporting systems, grievance procedures, and protection concepts, while also offering concrete help and emphasizing the responsibility of the perpetrators.

Here arises the question of what happens to perpetrators who become aware of their actions or wish to change their behavior, or admit to being perpetrators. A holistic approach must take this into account. While the severity of their actions should never be minimized or excused, the impact on them and their willingness to change must not be ignored.

Many perpetrators experience fear, especially when companies begin to address sexualized violence transparently. They fear for their reputation, professional standing, and career opportunities. Disciplinary actions threaten their professional position and lead to financial losses – a valid concern that prevents them from proactively addressing a transparent change in behavior. It often rather encourages them to openly oppose guidelines, training, and measures. The idea of being confronted with the consequences of their actions, whether publicly or internally, is also frightening. But it's not only that – perpetrators also fear social exclusion and ostracism if their actions come to light.

I AM A PERPETRATOR:
WHAT NOW?

When we realize that we have committed sexualized violence at the workplace, we initially feel insecure, intimidated, and ashamed. Often, we don't want to be a perpetrator.

Maybe we've made sexist jokes without realizing the potential vulnerability involved.
Maybe we've thought in stereotypes and feel cognitive dissonance.
Maybe we've only just realized that unequal pay for men and women is part of sexualized violence.
Perhaps we remember actions we've taken and want to avoid such situations in the future — as individuals or as companies.

This is the first step!

Almost everyone has made a comment that was perceived as inappropriate or hurtful at some point. Almost everyone has found themselves in a situation where their behavior unintentionally crossed boundaries. Almost everyone has held prejudices. Almost every company has hierarchies that promote unequal power relations. Almost every company has gender gaps. Almost every company has unequal promotion opportunities for different genders. It is important to become aware of this reality, as it opens the possibility for change through:

1. Reflection and Self-Criticism
Take time to reflect on your own actions and critically engage with your behavior. Try to understand how your actions may have hurt or harassed others.

2. Taking Responsibility
Accept responsibility for your actions and their consequences. Do not shift the responsibility onto others. Do not deny your guilt.

3. Apology and Regret
Seek opportunities to apologize sincerely to those affected – respectfully and honestly. Show real remorse for your actions and their effects.

4. Proactive Behavioral Change
Commit to changing your behavior and no longer tolerating sexualized violence at the workplace. Educate yourself on appropriate behavioral standards and make sure you follow them. Ask colleagues, friends, or advisors what about your behavior is inappropriate and how you can improve. Use feedback to implement changes and follow through.

5. Professional Support
Seek professional support to understand your behavioral patterns and work on them. A therapist or counselor can help you recognize deeper causes and achieve positive change. Continuing education, training, or coaching will expand your knowledge about sexualized violence and offer opportunities to learn and solidify alternative behaviors. There are specialized intervention programs for perpetrators that can support you. Counseling centers specializing in sexualized violence can be found under "Important Contacts" at the end of this book.

6. Participation in Measures and Prevention
Get involved in measures and programs aimed at prevention. Support the implementation of training, policies, and procedures that promote a safe and respectful working environment. While the healing

process for those affected takes precedence, your internal process is a key part of genuine change. Respect the needs of those affected for safety and privacy, and their decision on how and whether they wish to interact with you.

Your positive example encourages others to change their behavior. This reduces the risk of becoming abusive again in the future. By acquiring new communication, conflict resolution, and respectful behavior skills, you can also create a different sense of life for yourself. You can become more self-aware on a deeper level, perceive yourself more positively, and establish healthier relationships with yourself and others. Remember that change takes time.

You can do it!

A balanced approach that takes into account both the perspectives of the affected and the perpetrators leads to more revelations and more comprehensive solutions. And these are crucial because:

Sexualized violence makes people sick.

SEXUALIZED VIOLENCE MAKES PEOPLE SICK: NOT JUST THE VICTIMS

... but also teams and companies.

It poisons the working atmosphere and company culture. It demotivates, frightens, traumatizes, and causes massive impairments. The psychological and physical symptoms are diverse and can remain felt for a lifetime. From physical injuries to post-traumatic stress disorder, depression, addiction, and suicidal thoughts – the effects are profound and devastating.

Anna works in an office and is sexually harassed by a superior. He makes suggestive remarks, touches her inappropriately, and intimidates her. Anna is too scared to do anything about it, fearing the consequences and jeopardizing her job. The experience of sexualized violence deeply affects Anna and has far-reaching consequences on her life. She develops PTSD, suffers from depression and anxiety disorders, and struggles to trust others. Her self-esteem is severely impacted, and she wrestles with feelings of guilt and shame. Anna also faces difficulties advancing her career as the experience affects her work performance. Despite therapy and support, she carries the emotional and psychological scars of sexualized violence. Her colleagues make fun of her, saying she's not strong enough and imagining everything. Anna is trapped in a cycle of discrimination and blame.

Experiences like Anna's show that sexualized violence is no trivial matter and doesn't happen by chance. It is deliberately used and is often the result of socialized behaviors and institutional weaknesses. The psychological and physical symptoms triggered by this type of violence are diverse and felt for a lifetime.

To achieve violence-free workplaces, several building blocks must be considered. First, it is crucial to become aware of the structural embedding of sexualized violence. A nuanced and sensitized reporting process as well as transparent exchange are essential. Perpetrator-victim reversal, trivialization, and victim-blaming must be actively stopped. Instead, clear consequences for perpetrators are necessary. Civil courage serves as a role model to promote and live a culture of non-violence. Everyone can take a stand in their environment and with their individual means. By properly assessing risks, providing low-threshold and fast help, we contribute to stopping the spread of sexualized violence. Only when we perceive, look, take seriously, and respond, can we bring about positive change and foster a culture of non-violence.

Perceive! Look! Take seriously! React!

CHAPTER 5

ON THE TEST BENCH
THE COMPANIES

Sexualized violence in the workplace not only has serious consequences for the affected employees but also significant impacts on companies.

These impacts can be both financial and non-financial, encompassing direct as well as indirect costs.

Direct costs can involve legal liabilities and compensation claims, while indirect costs may include increased absenteeism, decreased productivity, and reputational damage that can hinder a company's long-term success and growth.

AN EXPENSIVE BURDEN:
COSTS FOR COMPANIES

The precise identification of these costs is difficult due to the lack of data. Several factors make it hard to determine the exact amount:

Unreported Cases
Sexualized violence at the workplace is often not reported because the victims fear stigmatization, career setbacks, or retaliation. Many incidents are thus not recorded and do not appear in cost statements, statistics, or studies.

Lack of (Standardized) Recording Methods
Different organizations use different categories and definitions, which leads to inconsistencies in the data. This complicates comparisons and the merging of data from various sources.

Privacy and Confidentiality
Many companies treat cases of sexualized violence confidentially, meaning the exact costs of individual cases or measures are not publicly known and do not appear in official reports.

Although the exact costs of sexualized violence at the workplace are not fully measurable, there is research on the costs of violence in Germany and Europe. From these studies, we can infer similar costs related to sexualized violence in the workplace.

Studies, such as one from EFFAT[42] (European Federation of Food, Agriculture, and Tourism) from 2011, estimate the annual costs in the European Union for gender-based violence against women at 228 billion euros, which corresponds to 1.8% of the EU's GDP. Of this, 45 billion euros are spent on public and state services, and 24 billion euros on lost economic productivity. A study from the European Institute for Gender Equality[43] (EIGE) in 2021 estimated the costs of gender-based violence in Europe at 366 billion euros per year. This is a 60% increase over 10 years! In Germany, the societal follow-up costs of domestic and sexualized violence against women amount to 54 billion euros per year, which equals approximately 148 million euros per day. These high costs arise, for example, in the healthcare system, police and justice sectors, and through absences from work. Only a negligible part of this amount is currently spent on public funding for support services, such as specialized counseling centers. To be more specific, even though this is not a reliable number, but one we've obtained from our own research and companies:

The cost per affected individual amounts to an average of €130,000 for a corporation.

At first glance, this may seem unbelievable.
However, when considering all parameters, this number seems quite plausible.

The economic costs are borne by the victims, employers, the state, and society, as shown by a 2019 report by Deloitte[44] for Australia. While Australia is not Germany, the study gives an impression of the costs incurred due to sexualized violence at the workplace. According to the report, 70% of the productivity losses are borne by companies, 23% of the emerging costs are covered by tax revenues, and 7% come from individual income losses. The largest share of productivity losses came from women in the age group 25-34 years, attributable to the high number of harassment cases in this group. According to the report, sexualized violence at the workplace in 2018 caused the following costs: $2.6 billion USD (approx. 2.4 billion euros) in productivity losses and $0.9 billion USD in other costs.

Each case results in a productivity loss of approximately 4 workdays.

The largest productivity loss comes from staff turnover (32% of the costs), which also leads to income losses, reduced profits, and lower tax payments. Significant losses also occur through absenteeism (28% of the costs) and the time spent addressing the cases (24% of the costs). Many companies are often unaware that sexualized violence also incurs significant expenses for them due to:

1. Legal Disputes

Companies face legal claims and proceedings, including lawsuits from victims and proceedings against perpetrators. These disputes incur high costs for lawyer fees, court costs, compensation claims, and fines.

2. Damage to Reputation

Sexualized violence in the workplace damages a company's reputation long-term. Negative media coverage by (former) employees in the media and networks, public pressure, and image problems result in the loss of talent, revenue, customers, business partners, and interest.

3. Turnover

Victims leave the company or develop mental health issues that reduce their productivity or lead to work incapacity. Often, not only the victims leave the company, but also other employees or partners who have witnessed the incidents or the company's inaction in response. This turnover results in costs for recruiting and onboarding new employees, disrupts operations, and burdens the work atmosphere.

4. Loss of Reputation and Brand Value
Companies that perform poorly in handling sexualized violence become deterrents. The loss of brand value and business opportunities are two of the consequences. In recent years, corporate branding regarding meaningfulness, commitment, and appreciation rise dramatically. Negative public reactions cause companies to lose reputation and market value.

Also, the costs for the affected employees are significant, as shown by a 2021 study by the Time's Up Foundation[45] for the USA:

1. Loss of Income
Many respondents lost income due to reduced shifts, missed promotions, and lost bonuses because their work performance was affected by the harassment or they were underutilized as retaliation for their reports.

2. Job Loss and Unemployment
Almost all respondents were unemployed for a period due to the traumatic experience, leading to significant direct costs. Often, the work environment became so hostile that victims were forced to leave the job.

3. Career Change and Delayed Promotion
Several women working in well-paid, male-dominated professions were reassigned to lower-paid roles, often in women-dominated sectors. This exacerbated career setbacks, the gender pay gap, role stereotypes, and normative statistics.

4. Performance Loss
Losing jobs led not only to income losses but also to the loss of valuable benefits, such as pension contributions, health care, and allowances.

5. Medical Fees and Co-pays
Treating the physical and psychological aftermath incurred high costs, especially when healing services were not fully covered by health insurance.

6. Career Change
A forced career change, retraining, or necessary new qualifications also caused significant expenses, including tuition and material costs, as well as opportunity costs for the time spent learning.

7. Follow-up Damage or Costs
A lower income has negative impacts on personal finances, including credit defaults, lower credit ratings, insecure housing situations, or garnished assets.

Prevention, on the other hand, significantly strengthens personal safety, as well as corporate productivity, innovation, and economic power!
Estimates[46] suggest that global GDP would rise by about 15% if women, for example, participated equally in economic life.

It is, therefore, also financially time for a cultural change.

CULTURAL CHANGE: IMPACT ON MOTIVATION

Sexualized violence at the workplace has far-reaching negative effects on the entire environment. A climate of fear, distrust, and insecurity emerges, which severely impairs collaboration, team spirit, and the work atmosphere. The consequences for motivation, performance, and productivity are significant. Instead of focusing on their actual tasks, employees must defend themselves against attacks and endure abuse of power.

Other people in the work environment are also insecure and spend their energy on correctly assessing or avoiding situations. Responsible contact persons are more occupied with handling cases than with preventive work. All of this generates additional stress, pressure, and disruptions. Reduced concentration, lower performance, and diminished engagement are just a few of the possible consequences.

Moreover, employee satisfaction suffers significantly. When workplace pressures are high, well-being with work and the work environment decreases. Dissatisfied employees tend to be less engaged, creative, helpful, loyal, and healthy.

Companies whose workforce is less engaged, creative, helpful, loyal, and healthy often experience a decline in productivity, higher turnover, and increased sick leaves, leading to even more dissatisfaction, more stress, absences, and so on for the remaining staff. A self-perpetuating cycle that is lethal for companies.

TAKING RESPONSIBILITY: FROM THE COMPANIES' PERSPECTIVE

Companies are therefore faced with the challenge of implementing measures to prevent sexualized violence at the workplace and effective intervention strategies, while simultaneously maintaining their economic viability. Proven building blocks are:

1. Prevention Measures

Comprehensive behavioral guidelines that strictly prohibit sexualized violence in any form at the workplace and define clear consequences for violations are crucial. It is equally important to sensitize all involved parties to respectful behavior and inform them about behavioral standards. Effective mechanisms for reporting incidents that ensure all cases are taken seriously and dealt with appropriately are also essential. Regular training creates continuous awareness of the issue and empowers employees to deal with inappropriate behavior and violent situations.

2. Promoting a Positive Workplace Culture

An inclusive workplace culture that promotes diversity, equality, and respect is achieved through targeted support for networks and project groups. These initiatives create an environment where everyone feels valued and heard, prejudices are reduced, and equal opportunities are promoted.

3. Training

Training for employees and leaders on recognition, prevention, and intervention can be offered in various attractive formats, such as in-person seminars, online modules, or workshops with external experts. When the content is regularly updated and repeated, it ensures long-term effectiveness and keeps all parties informed. Through continuous training, organizations lay a strong foundation for a respectful and safe work environment and ensure that everyone knows how to appropriately respond to incidents and, ideally, prevent them.

Such short-term investments pay off in the long run, as they reduce costs for companies, improve the work environment, and make the corporate culture more attractive. A Code of Conduct helps to recognize and respond to discrimination, foster a common language, prevent abuse, maintain boundaries, and ensure respectful communication. The result is fewer complaints and conflicts, a safe work environment, and respectful interactions—also regarding other dimensions of discrimination such as homophobia, ableism, ageism, racism, and all other aspects of discrimination.

Such a commitment to prevention and respect not only strengthens the corporate culture but ultimately the long-term success of the company.

ACTING TOGETHER:
FROM THE EMPLOYEES' PERSPECTIVE

Prevention and intervention are not only important from a business perspective but also for the employees, as they ensure:

Protection
Working in a safe and respectful environment without fear of harassment, discrimination, or violence provides great value.

Well-being and Productivity
Through mental and physical well-being, everyone feels more satisfied, in a better mood, collaborates better, and increases innovation and productivity.

Inclusive Workplace Culture
A company that respects, appreciates, and accepts everyone in their diversity creates a positive work environment and strengthens collaboration within teams and as a whole.

Equality and Equal Opportunity
Structural and financial equality signal that everyone is equally challenged and supported.

Empowerment
Knowing one's rights and opportunities empowers and encourages standing up for oneself and others - no ifs or buts.

CHAPTER 6

ON THE TEST BENCH
POLITICS

Every person has the fundamental – also legal – right to remain unharmed and unscathed in all encounters.

And this applies privately, in public, in personal or virtual interactions, on the phone or in social networks, in magazines, films, advertising, or entertainment.

And in the workplace!

FOCUS:
LEGAL FOUNDATIONS

Every person deserves respectful and fair treatment. It is the responsibility of political decision-makers and systems to implement rights that create work environments where sexualized violence is not tolerated. Therefore, sexualized violence or "sexual harassment" in Germany is prohibited by several laws, including:

General Equal Treatment Act
The General Equal Treatment Act is the central anti-discrimination law in Germany and prohibits discrimination based on various characteristics, including gender. It contains specific provisions on "sexual harassment" in the workplace and obligates employers to take measures to prevent and stop such incidents. At the same time, it protects employees from negative consequences if they report "sexual harassment." The Act ensures that affected individuals can report grievances in a safe environment without fearing reprisals.

Occupational Safety Act
The Occupational Safety Act protects employees from hazards at the workplace, including psychological stress. "Sexual harassment" and other forms of sexualized violence can be considered psychological stress, which must be prevented according to the Occupational Safety Act.

Law on the Convention No. 190 of the International Labour Organization of June 21, 2019, on the Elimination of Violence and Harassment in the World of Work
On December 21, 2022, the federal cabinet approved the bill to ratify Convention No. 190 of the International

Labour Organization (ILO) of 2019. The convention sends a global signal that any behavior that humiliates, degrades, sexually harasses, or physically or psychologically attacks people at the workplace is prohibited and condemned. It applies to both employees and natural persons in employer functions.

Pay Transparency Act
This law promotes transparency regarding pay equality between men and women. It requires companies to disclose their salary structures and allows employees to access information about pay structures. While primarily focused on pay equality, it indirectly contributes to creating a fairer work environment by counteracting inequality.

Works Constitution Act
This law regulates the rights and obligations of works councils and contains provisions for combating sexualized violence in the workplace. Works councils have the right to demand and enforce measures to protect employees.

Collective Agreements and Company Agreements
Collective agreements or company agreements contain regulations for the prevention and combating of sexualized violence. They often offer additional protection measures beyond the legal requirements.

Directive on the Implementation of the Principle of Equal Opportunities and Equal Treatment of Men and Women in Employment and Occupation
The EU Directive 2006/54/EC of the European Parliament and Council of July 5, 2006, on the implementation of the principle of equal opportunities and equal treatment of men and women in employment and occupation

prohibits "sexual harassment" in the workplace and obligates member states to take appropriate measures.

Directive on Minimum Standards for the Rights, Support, and Protection of Victims of Crime

The EU Directive 2012/29/EU of the European Parliament and Council of October 25, 2012, on minimum standards for the rights, support, and protection of victims of crime also covers sexual violence in the workplace and sets minimum standards for the protection and support of affected individuals.

Equality of Men and Women in Access to and the Supply of Goods and Services

The EU Directive 2004/113/EC aims to prevent discrimination based on gender in access to and the supply of goods and services. Although primarily focused on access to services and goods, it promotes the principle of equality and protects against gender-based discrimination in various areas, including the workplace.

Equal Opportunities and Equal Treatment of Men and Women in Employment and Occupation

The EU Directive 2006/54/EC prohibits "sexual harassment" and sets the requirements for gender equality in relation to employment and working conditions. It requires employers to take measures to prevent gender discrimination and promote equal opportunities.

Reconciliation of Work and Family Life for Parents and Caregivers

The EU Directive 2019/1158/EU promotes the reconciliation of work and family life by creating better working conditions for parents and caregivers. By improving working conditions for specific groups, it indirectly contributes to creating a more just and respectful work environment.

Rights, Support, and Protection of Victims of Crime
The EU Directive 2012/29/EU sets minimum standards for the rights, support, and protection of victims of crime, including sexualized violence. It emphasizes the need to comprehensively support affected individuals and provide access to protection and support services.

By implementing and adhering to these and other directives, companies ensure that some basic foundations are laid in the fight against discrimination and sexualized violence.

(NO) COURAGE FOR THE GAP:
IMPLEMENTATION AND ENFORCEMENT OF LAWS

Legal protective measures in Germany are still not conclusive. There are still challenges and issues in the implementation and enforcement. It is therefore crucial that companies establish appropriate procedures and ensure effective protection.

Courage for the gap is not appropriate here.

However, there are gaps in legal protection in Germany. These particularly include:

Difficulties in Proof
Affected individuals often have difficulty legally proving the incident. It can be complicated to find witnesses or secure evidence, especially in cases of verbal or non-physical harassment.

Different Standards
There are no uniform standards for dealing with sexualized violence in the workplace, which leads to uncertainty and inconsistency.

Lack of Sanctions
It is challenging to establish and enforce appropriate sanctions for perpetrators. Often, the punishments are not sufficiently deterrent or transparent enough to prevent further acts.

Legal reforms and improvements are still needed for more effectiveness. But what exactly is needed?

Effective Consequences for Perpetrators
Current sanctions need to be reviewed and adjusted to ensure they are deterrent and applied consistently. Perpetrators must feel the consequences of their actions and be held accountable.

Uniform Guidelines
Clear and uniform standards are needed across all industries. Consistency and transparency are essential to reduce confusion and uncertainty and provide clear guidance.

Better Support for Affected Individuals
Affected individuals need more comprehensive support, through specialized counseling services, psychosocial support, and financial compensation. A system is needed that encourages affected persons and provides the necessary protection and help.

Prevention as a Priority
Prevention is the best protection against sexualized violence in the workplace. And education is the best prevention. Legal reforms should also include increased awareness-raising and protective measures. Concrete measures for employees and leadership responsibilities must be demanded to raise awareness of the issue and find solutions.

Effective Reporting Mechanisms
Affected individuals must feel safe to report incidents easily and at low threshold – both internally and externally. Legal reforms should therefore provide clear and effective reporting mechanisms that are confidential, accessible, and trustworthy. Open communication and real protection from negative consequences are crucial.

Regular Review and Adjustment

Protection mechanisms must be continuously reflected upon and improved. Legal reforms should include regular reviews and adjustments to ensure that the protective measures remain effective and meet the changing needs and challenges. This should also involve the interdisciplinary inclusion of contact persons, affected individuals, perpetrators, and other actors.

WHERE WE STAND: GERMANY IN COMPARISON

In comparison to Europe, women in Germany experience harassment at the workplace most frequently.

This is shown by the survey "European Observatory on Sexism and Sexual Harassment at Work" by the Brussels-based Foundation for European Progressive Studies (FEPS) in collaboration with the French Fondation Jean-Jaurès[47]. The study surveyed a total of 5,000 women, with about 1,000 in Italy, Spain, France, the United Kingdom, and Germany, about their experiences. According to the survey, 68% of the women surveyed in Germany have experienced sexualized violence at the workplace, just like 66% of working women in Spain, 57% in the UK, 56% in Italy, and 55% in France.

Sexualized violence in the workplace is therefore a topic that affects not only Germany but is also widespread in other European countries[48]. Legal regulations and practices vary in European countries despite a basic harmonization through EU directives. Let's take a look beyond the country borders:

United Kingdom

Equality Act 2010
Includes all forms of unwanted sexual behavior that violates dignity or creates a hostile, degrading, or offensive environment.
Employers are liable for actions of their employees, even if they did not authorize them. Employers are expected to take proactive measures, such as clear policies and training.
It is not necessary for the unwanted behavior to be labeled as such in advance. Employers can defend

themselves by proving that all reasonable steps to prevent the abuse were taken.

Italy

Code of Equal Opportunities (Law No. 198/2006)
"Sexual harassment" is a form of discrimination and includes unwanted sexual behavior that violates dignity or creates a hostile working environment.
Employers have the duty to take measures to protect against "sexual harassment" and ensure that such incidents are reported and punished.
Employers can be held liable even if they are not directly responsible, due to their obligation to ensure the health and safety of the workforce.

France

"Sexual harassment" is a criminal offense in France.
Employers are required to take swift and effective action when complaints arise. They must conduct immediate investigations into any allegations of sexual harassment and implement protective measures to shield the affected individuals from further harassment. Failure to respond appropriately can result in legal consequences for the employer. If sexual harassment is proven, the perpetrator must be dismissed, and the employer may face legal action and compensation claims for not acting.
Employers are also obligated to provide training on the prevention of sexual harassment within the company, ensure that affected individuals have access to psychological support, and establish an anonymous complaint system. These measures ensure that victims feel safe and supported when reporting incidents.

Repeated behavior or conversations of a sexual nature that violate dignity or create a hostile work environment are strictly prohibited.

Denmark

Act on Equal Treatment of Men and Women
Similar to the EU definition, this includes direct sexual behavior such as touching and unwanted sexual advances.
Employers must act when they learn of "sexual harassment," but there are no specific legal requirements for the investigation procedure.
There are no legal obligations for the prevention of "sexual harassment," but large companies often implement policies and training.

Belgium

Laws on psychosocial risks, including "sexual harassment"
"Sexual harassment" is considered part of the general regulations on psychosocial risks.
Employers must take measures based on a risk assessment and provide an internal complaints office as well as psychological support.
Employers risk criminal and civil consequences if they do not comply with regulations. It is advised to investigate the allegations and take disciplinary measures if necessary.

Germany

General Equal Treatment Act (of 2006, amended by Article 4 of the Act of December 19, 2022 (BGBl. I S. 2510).

"Sexual harassment" is defined as a form of gender-based discrimination. It includes unwanted sexual actions, comments, or gestures that violate the dignity of the affected person or create a hostile, degrading, or offensive environment. Employers are required to take appropriate measures to protect employees from sexual harassment and to promote a discrimination-free workplace culture. This includes developing and implementing anti-harassment policies, conducting regular training for employees, and establishing a complaint system. Employers must take immediate action and conduct an internal investigation when a complaint is received. In cases of confirmed sexual harassment, they are obligated to take appropriate measures, ranging from warnings to dismissals. Additionally, employers must protect the affected person from further harassment. They can be held liable for damages if they fail to meet their duty to prevent harassment.

Not only are there differences in rights and obligations across Europe – the figures regarding gender equality also vary: In 2022, Denmark achieved the best score for gender equality in the European Union (EU)[49] with an index of 0.01 according to the Gender Inequality Index (GII). In contrast, Cyprus showed the highest degree of gender-specific inequality within the EU with a GII of around 0.25. Germany, with a GII of about 0.07, ranks in the middle and shows moderate progress in gender equality compared to other EU countries. Ahead of Germany are Sweden, the Netherlands, Finland, Luxembourg, Belgium,

Austria, Slovenia, Spain, and Italy.
When it comes to gender equality in leadership positions, the picture is different. On average across the EU[50], just over one-third of leaders were women in 2023 (35.2%). In Sweden, women held 44.3% of leadership positions, the highest share among all EU member states and candidate countries. Germany, with a share of around 29% female leaders, was below the EU-wide average. At the bottom of the EU ranking was Luxembourg, where fewer than one in four leadership positions were held by women.

Women who are politically active and sit in parliaments also experience sexualized violence. In the 2018[51] survey "Sexism, harassment and violence against women parliamentarians" by the Inter-Parliamentary Union, 20% of the women surveyed reported being sexually harassed during their time in parliament. 7.3% reported that someone had attempted to coerce them into sexual relationships. Others referred to inappropriate and unwanted gestures, such as touching breasts or buttocks. These actions usually took place in parliament, at political meetings, at official dinners, workshops, or trips abroad. The respondents reported that most of these actions were committed by male colleagues, from both opposition and government parties.

The implementation and effectiveness of laws, policies, commitments, and regulations are influenced by cultural norms, political circumstances, and social conditions. Nevertheless, other European countries have made progress that Germany can use as a guide. Germany can and will benefit from these experiences.

CHAPTER 7

ON THE TEST BENCH
SOCIETY

Sexualized violence in the workplace is a personal drama for the affected individuals.

However, as outlined in the previous chapters, sexualized violence also has significant economic and financial consequences for companies and all involved parties.

From absenteeism and sick leave to performance losses, career setbacks, legal costs, and health issues – the impacts are diverse and far-reaching for all.

THE DARK CONSEQUENCES: TANGIBLE IMPACTS

The consequences go far beyond the already discussed personal and corporate aspects. The societal impacts of sexualized violence in the workplace are equally alarming.

Companies that tolerate sexualized violence or fail to respond appropriately normalize unacceptable behavior through inaction or lack of consequences. This has far-reaching consequences for our societal norms and values. It affects gender equality, undermines workplace appreciation, and reinforces problematic patterns in areas such as advertising and compensation.

If companies do not take consistent action against sexualized violence, they contribute to the entrenchment of harmful social rules and structures that negatively affect the entire societal climate. The acceptance of actions and the simultaneous lack of consequences strengthen the culture of silence and immunity for the perpetrators, hindering the urgently needed progress.

CAUGHT IN STEREOTYPES: (UN)CONSCIOUS BIAS

"You're so bitchy – are you on your period?"

"Please make the coffee, that's what you're here for as a woman!"

"You, a man in nursing?! Why don't you become a doctor?"

Have you ever heard or thought such things?

Even though we may not want to, our attitudes are often the result of our socialization, which is still largely shaped by biased gender roles. Therefore, it is not surprising that there is a strong connection between sexualized violence and stereotypical structures. Sexualized violence is often the result of deeply rooted gender inequalities and discriminations in various areas.

An act carried out by a woman often does not have the same impact as the same action committed by a man. Is it because women are not expected to commit such acts? Or because "men don't experience such things"? Or are we particularly unsettled and overwhelmed when women step out of traditional gender roles and act aggressively, violently, or inconsiderately instead of with care, sensitivity, and empathy?

Yes, these are also reasons.
There are many aspects rooted in our biases: In many societies, men are generally overrepresented in positions of power or power structures. The impacts of sexualized violence are often linked to these power dynamics. Male perpetrators are often perceived as threats who act out of a claim to power or domi-

nance, while female perpetrators are less frequently associated with these power structures and are perceived as less threatening, even when they commit violence. This leads to sexualized violence by women being taken less seriously or even seen as less harmful.

This imbalance also explains the widespread acceptance of verbal forms of sexualized violence, particularly against women. Many women are also unaware that such behavior may be criminal and have a destructive impact on their self-esteem, autonomy, and self-confidence. As a result, women tend to downplay incidents of sexualized violence:

"That was just a slip-up..."

"I shouldn't be so sensitive."

"I probably just misunderstood..."

The results of a 2022 Ipsos Global study[52] also highlight how widespread outdated thinking patterns regarding gender roles still are. Stereotypes that portray women as weak, passive, or helpless often lead to the victims being blamed or held responsible. The idea that women provoke harassment or attacks through their behavior, clothing, or appearance shifts the blame onto the women themselves, rather than holding the perpetrators accountable. Other role models that objectify women as sexual objects, as sexually available, or as rewards for men, contribute to viewing sexual harassment as normal or acceptable – almost as an inevitable part of interpersonal relationships.

The notion that women are less capable of defending themselves contributes to women projecting the blame for sexual assaults onto themselves or hesitating to resist. When women are also only socially acknowledged when they are "decent," "pure," or "innocent," those affected by sexualized violence often feel shame or guilt – because they often feel used, guilty, and sullied. Combined with the idea that women "didn't deserve it" or "provoked it," this leads to further shame and silence about their experiences. The still widespread gender stereotypes and traditional role expectations foster a culture of violence – accepted and normalized.

Not only traditional ideas about women's roles contribute to the perpetuation of sexualized violence. Stereotypical views about men downplay or excuse actions. The idea that men are dominant, aggressive, and assertive denies that they can also be victims of sexualized violence. After all, "real men" should be able to defend themselves. All others are simply "not strong enough." Men also struggle to speak out about their own experiences with sexualized violence or seek help, out of fear of being seen as "unmanly" or "too weak."

Additionally, normative views about LGBTQIA+ people contribute to the perpetuation of sexualized violence and discrimination. Prejudices such as the assumption that LGBTQIA+ individuals are "provocative" or "inappropriate" due to their sexual orientation or gender identity promote the idea that these individuals are responsible for the harassment or discrimination they face. These prejudices lead to the experiences of violence or discrimination against the LGBTQIA+ community being dismissed or minimized. Further prejudices, like the belief that LGBTQIA+ individuals are "isolated cases" or "not really affected" by violence, also contribute to marginalization and stigmatization. And these views are not only wrong but also dangerous.

As a society and as individuals, we must recognize that such stereotyping not only has negative effects on the affected individuals but also contributes to maintaining a climate of violence and discrimination. These prejudices not only cause injustices but also prevent us from creating a fairer and more respectful environment.

It is high time to dismantle our prejudices. To do this, we must first become aware of them.

TURNING OFF AUTOPILOT: FROM UNCONSCIOUS TO CONSCIOUS

Unconscious bias refers to cognitive perception distortions of which we are unaware. These distortions arise in connection with stereotypes, prejudices, and societal discrimination processes. They affect our judgment, decision-making, and actions. Unconscious biases can influence personnel selection decisions and performance evaluations, enable or end careers. Even if we believe we are being objective and fair, we unconsciously act with bias, thus reinforcing inequality of opportunity and social injustice.

Unconscious biases affect our mental perceptions and thinking processes, our decisions and actions – almost on autopilot. And this occurs in various contexts, such as fairness and justice, effective collaboration, trust and conflict resolution, fostering innovation and diversity of ideas, as well as personal development. To turn off your autopilot, you can use different methods:

Reflect
Regularly reflect on your thoughts, assumptions, and reactions. Ask yourself why you think or act a certain way, and question your own (pre)judices.

Acquire knowledge
Inform yourself about the different types of biases and how they can affect your thinking and behavior. Knowledge helps sharpen your awareness.

Give and receive feedback
Others can help you recognize unconscious biases. Take responsibility for your own biases and actively work to overcome them.

Change perspectives

Engage with people from different backgrounds, cultures, opinions, and life experiences – both in your personal and professional environment.

Show empathy

Put yourself in the shoes of others and understand their perceptions. This will help dismantle prejudices and foster a curious and understanding attitude.

Network

Find allies and form a network. Together, you can support each other and contribute to creating a more inclusive environment.

To find out how consciously and unbiasedly you are thinking and acting, you can ask yourself self-reflective questions:

The self-reflection questionnaire

1. Are you open to the diversity of people around you?

2. Do you actively listen and respect others' opinions, even if they differ from your own?

3. Do you show empathy and try to put yourself in others' shoes?

4. Do you create equal opportunities for people of different genders?

5. Do you ensure that your actions respect the dignity and boundaries of your colleagues and employees?

6. Do you use inclusive language and avoid discriminatory expressions?

7. Do you actively advocate for equality, justice, and fairness?

8. Do you recognize and question biases and stereotypes?

9. Do you create an environment where everyone feels safe and respected?

10. Do you promote a culture of openness in which sexualized violence can be discussed?

A CHANGE IS NECESSARY:
THE IMPORTANCE OF TRANSFORMATION

Social change is crucial.

By raising awareness in ourselves and others, we generate direct and indirect changes. This requires a fundamental transformation of attitudes and norms that have tolerated or supported sexualized violence. Companies must send clear messages and establish zero-tolerance cultures. Public pressure and awareness-raising are crucial for improving laws and guidelines. We need models for orientation and as role models. It is therefore high time for a few encouraging examples:

Volkswagen

Since 1996, Volkswagen has actively fought against discrimination in the workplace. Through targeted measures, it is made clear that "sexual harassment" and other forms of discrimination are serious violations. The works agreement defines clear guidelines for dealing with "sexual harassment," bullying, and other discriminations. Volkswagen informs about active participation opportunities, counseling services, and complaint procedures. Regular training for leadership and HR responsibilities, as well as works councils, complements the measures and makes the topic visible.

Charité Berlin

Charité Berlin has been actively engaged in combating "sexual harassment," especially in the medical and nursing sectors, since 2013. Charité Berlin draws clear boundaries between professional behavior and unwanted boundary violations and provides information and practical tips on counseling, complaint procedures, and legal foundations.

Time´s Up

The Time's Up movement in the USA is particularly committed to combating sexualized violence in the entertainment industry. The initiative, initiated by women from various industries, advocates for concrete changes, equal opportunities, and the protection of employees from sexual harassment. Time's Up has set new standards for the entertainment industry, but its reach also benefits all professional sectors.

Uber

Uber has also recognized that a cultural shift is necessary and has learned from it. Following allegations of sexualized violence by employees, the company has introduced comprehensive training and workshops, established clear behavioral guidelines, and improved incident reporting mechanisms. In addition, women and underrepresented groups have been actively appointed to leadership positions to foster a more inclusive corporate culture.

Microsoft

In recent years, Microsoft has also taken more decisive actions to combat sexualized violence in the workplace.

With employee training, improved reporting mechanisms, and independent investigation processes, the company has set clear standards and fostered a culture of openness and transparency.

These companies show that change is possible.
Yes, it requires continuous effort, engaging with complex issues, and the courage to challenge prevailing standards.
But it's time for companies to take responsibility and ensure a safe and respectful work environment.
And to present themselves as role models and multipliers.

It's worth it!

NAME IT

CHAPTER 8

PERPETRATORS
TYPICAL PATTERNS OF OFFENSE

Recognizing sexualized violence is the first step toward prevention. Naming this violence represents the second step.

However, naming it is often hindered by fears of false accusations, reputational damage, or legal consequences.

Victims frequently encounter skepticism and doubt about their statements, which is often rooted in the myth of false accusations.

FACING THE FACTS:
THE ISSUE OF FALSE ACCUSATIONS

Studies at the European and German levels estimate the proportion of false accusations in reported rape cases to be between 1% and 9%, with an average of about 3%.

These figures are significantly lower than commonly assumed. This is partly because media coverage of false accusations has received disproportionately high attention. As a result, the impression arises that such false allegations occur more frequently than they actually do. Headlines dealing with the supposed innocence of suspects or the exposure of false accusations are sensational and spread quickly. However, they distort perception and lead to an overrepresentation of false allegations. In contrast, most actual cases of sexualized violence receive little to no media coverage. This results in the frequency and severity of undeniable acts of sexualized violence being significantly underrepresented in public perception.

When women accuse men of sexualized violence, society often reacts with skepticism. Immediately, reasons and motives are sought to question the allegations:

> *"Could it be that the sex was consensual, but the woman later regretted it and therefore claimed it was rape?"*

> *"Could she be accusing her ex-partner of rape out of revenge because he cheated on or left her?"*

> *"Or is she just seeking attention?"*

Scientific studies and articles on rape and criminal prosecution clearly show how distorted societal perception is. Depending on the study, country, interpreting person, and political perspective, the proportion of false accusations varies. The German Federal Association of Women's Counseling Centers and Women's Emergency Hotlines estimates the proportion in Germany to be 3%.

There are also different terms used in the interpretation of studies and legal terminology: False accusation, false report, wrongful suspicion, and false testimony. The German Criminal Code (StGB) differentiates between various legal contexts for false accusations:

Paragraph § 164 StGB
addresses "wrongful suspicion" and punishes individuals who knowingly falsely accuse another person to initiate official proceedings against them.

Paragraph § 153 StGB
concerns "false testimony under oath" in court.

Paragraph § 154 StGB
deals with "perjury" in the context of sworn statements.

Paragraph § 145d StGB
Punishes the "fabrication of a crime" when someone deliberately pretends that a crime has occurred to trigger an investigation.

However, statistics only record cases where a criminal proceeding is initiated for one of these offenses. False statements or accusations that do not lead to criminal proceedings are not documented. Although the German Police Crime Statistics (PKS) include a category like "fabrication of a crime against sexual self-determination," this covers a broad spectrum of offenses. Moreover, a large proportion of sexualized violence goes unreported, meaning these studies only capture the "visible cases" - those that are reported. A study by the German Federal Ministry for Family Affairs, Senior Citizens, Women, and Youth[53] estimates that over 85% of cases go unreported. This hidden figure significantly reduces the proportion of potential false accusations. Additionally, reports are less frequently filed against perpetrators known to the victim than against strangers: 50% of reports concern strangers, while only 18% of reports are against acquaintances.

It is therefore crucial that identifying boundary-violating behavior and reporting sexualized violence is taken seriously and freed from prejudices and false assumptions. There needs to be awareness of the high number of unreported cases and the barriers that prevent victims from coming forward. Only through a differentiated and sensitive approach can we contribute to recognizing, naming, and effectively combating sexualized violence. One important aspect is understanding that someone who makes a false accusation is committing a criminal offense that can be legally prosecuted. False accusations arise for various reasons. In many cases, there is a personal or intimate relationship between the accuser and the accused:

Misunderstandings
False accusations can stem from misunderstandings or misinterpretations of actions or statements.

Revenge or Retaliation
False accusations are sometimes made out of revenge or retaliation for personal grievances, breakups, or conflicts in relationships. They can be a means of harming the accused or provoking an emotional response.

Cover-up

False accusations can be an attempt to cover up inappropriate actions or divert attention from one's own mistakes. For example, this may happen when the accuser has something to hide or when both individuals were involved in an illicit relationship that, if exposed, could cause trouble for the accuser. In such cases, they may resort to false accusations to retroactively frame the relationship as abuse and portray themselves as blameless.

Mental Health Issues

People experiencing psychological distress may struggle to distinguish between their perceptions and actual events. This can lead to false accusations or distorted representations of their experiences. However, this does not mean that people with mental illnesses are generally unreliable! These cases are exceptions. It is always essential to balance protecting victims' rights with a thorough examination of accusations.

Social Pressure

Societal expectations can push individuals toward making false accusations if they feel that doing so aligns them with social norms or expectations.

Although false accusations are rare, they have severe consequences for those affected. They lead to significant emotional and psychological distress, damage or destroy trust in the community and workplace, and result in legal and social consequences. The stigma and social pressure associated with such allegations can have a long-lasting negative impact on the falsely accused person's life.

Moreover, false accusations do not help actual victims of sexualized violence; instead, they contribute to further stigmatization. Rather than improving the situation, they worsen the burden and injustice for those who are already suffering. Therefore, the key is: Objectivity instead of criminalization!

FACTUALITY INSTEAD OF CRIMINALIZATION: OBJECTIVE NOT SUBJECTIVE

Before legal or criminal measures are taken, a thorough and impartial review of the facts is required.

What does this mean in practice?

When witnessing an incident, suspecting misconduct, or facing a concrete situation, it is crucial to describe it objectively to avoid premature judgments and defamation.

It was a normal day at the office when Ayla observed a situation that made her uncomfortable. She saw and heard her colleague Haruto make an inappropriate remark and gesture toward their colleague Sarah. It was not the first time she had noticed such behavior from Haruto, but this time, she decided to take action. But how should she proceed without putting herself at risk, overstepping boundaries, falsely accusing her colleague, overwhelming Sarah, or putting herself in a difficult position?

Ayla's example illustrates that observations and suspicions primarily trigger uncertainty. It is advisable to talk to trusted colleagues or professional counseling services to gain clarity about the observed behavior and the next steps. Even though it may be difficult, such discussions are important to avoid either premature judgments or trivialization. Instead, they help find appropriate wording and approaches that align with one's experience and contribute to clarification. Contacting a specialized counseling service is not the same as filing a police report; rather, it serves as personal support and fact-finding. To ensure a thorough investigation that benefits all parties involved - including the affected person, the observer, the responsible contact person, legal representatives, and the accused - it is essential to consider the following aspects:

Objective Examination of Evidence
Before an individual faces employment-related or criminal consequences, all available evidence and information must be thoroughly and objectively examined. Subjective impressions or emotional reactions are not a valid basis for legal decisions.

Impartial Assessment
Allegations are evaluated without bias or preconceived opinions. All relevant information and perspectives are taken into account to ensure a fair and just assessment.

Avoiding Premature Judgments
The investigation remains neutral and unbiased to ensure that every person receives a fair process. No one should be prematurely judged or stigmatized based on accusations alone.

Consideration of All Perspectives
Both the accuser's and the accused's statements are heard and placed in context. The process follows the multi-eyes principle, involving multiple individuals to ensure diverse perspectives are considered as objectively as possible.

Professional Support
Consultants and legally trained professionals ensure that the situation is assessed correctly and professionally. This enables decisions based on solid and objective foundations

Maintaining Proportionality

The measures and actions taken in response to an allegation must be proportionate and appropriate. Decisions should not be based on speculation or incomplete information but on well-founded and expert assessments.

Actual assaults must be named and reported, even if they initially seem minor. Studies on offenders and their strategies have shown that they often manipulate boundaries and social dynamics through seemingly insignificant actions to remain undetected. Therefore, even seemingly minor incidents should be reported to prevent false accusations while ensuring that actual offenses are properly addressed.

Employers have a dual responsibility: They have a duty of care and protection toward all employees. In the event of a complaint, they may be held liable for damages if they fail to adequately protect the affected person. At the same time, they must ensure an objective investigation and impose proportional sanctions against the accused to avoid legal consequences.

Balancing these responsibilities and identifying perpetrators requires knowledge of offense patterns and dynamics.

BREAKING THE CYCLE:
IDENTIFYING PERPETRATORS

Have you ever noticed colleagues repeatedly making subtle remarks that, when taken together, create an uncomfortable work atmosphere? Have there been situations where supervisors overstepped employees' boundaries or made inappropriate comments that were not adequately addressed? Have you perhaps observed recurring tactics used by perpetrators, such as the deliberate exploitation of power dynamics or the creation of isolated situations?

Or has your company already taken steps to prevent such situations? Perhaps workshops have been organized to raise awareness of the signs of sexualized violence. Does your organization have clear policies and procedures for reporting and investigating incidents? Are informational materials regularly provided?

By asking yourself these questions, you can identify and adjust structures and strategies that may either enable or prevent such acts. There are typical patterns in cases of sexualized violence in the workplace, such as:

Familiarity in the Workplace
Often, those affected, bystanders, and perpetrators know each other from the professional environment, which makes uncovering and dealing with such incidents more difficult.

Relationships of Trust or Dependence
Acts frequently occur in situations where there is a relationship of trust or dependence—whether through hierarchies, team affiliations, biases, or obligations within the workplace.

Loyalty

Loyalty toward the perpetrator or the company often exists, making it harder to report, disclose, or process the incident.

Exploiting Positions of Power

Perpetrators often abuse their power or create such positions to manipulate, pressure, or intimidate others.

Use of Spatial Conditions

Spatial conditions are often deliberately used to conceal assaults.

Tabooing

When the topic is taboo, the willingness to speak about it or report incidents decreases.

Inducing Feelings of Guilt

Victims are often made to feel that they provoked or wanted the assault through their behavior. This makes investigations more difficult and silences those affected.

These patterns highlight how deeply rooted and complex the issue is in the workplace. It requires a sensitive and comprehensive approach. Sexualized violence is rarely a single, clear-cut assault but rather develops over time. However, by recognizing this process and the enabling dynamics early on, we can stop it.

Perpetrators take advantage of favorable structures and invest significant time in shaping their outward appearance. You likely do not suspect most people you know of violent acts - and in most cases, this assumption is correct.

However, perpetrators often present themselves as open and

approachable, sharing personal aspects of their lives to build trust. Some are seen as exemplary employees, highly respected, or even indispensable within the company. This makes addressing sexualized violence committed by such individuals particularly difficult.

Additionally, perpetrators gradually push boundaries. They test how others react to their behavior, build on that knowledge, and adjust their actions accordingly. Anyone can be affected, as perpetrators do not always select their targets based on fixed criteria; they also exploit situational factors or existing power dynamics.

It is therefore crucial that companies actively recognize, communicate, and respond to this issue.

THE DARVO TACTIC:
PERPETRATORS' STRATEGIES

A common pattern used by perpetrators is the DARVO strategy. DARVO, a term coined by American psychologist Dr. Jennifer J. Freyd, stands for "Deny, Attack, and Reverse Victim and Offender." This manipulation tactic is designed to deny responsibility, attack the victim, and reverse the roles of victim and perpetrator.

Deny
Perpetrators using this tactic first deny the act, claiming that the misconduct never took place.

Attack
They then attack the victim, undermining their credibility or accusing them of provocation or shared responsibility.

Reverse Victim and Offender
Finally, they swap roles, portraying themselves as the victim while framing the actual victim as the perpetrator.

This strategy further harms those affected, making them feel unheard and discredited. DARVO poses a significant challenge to addressing and resolving incidents, as it distorts the narrative and undermines support. It is all the more important to recognize and counteract DARVO. Only through a deep understanding and awareness of this tactic can the protection of victims and the effective handling of such cases be ensured. Identifying the dynamics of DARVO is essential to correctly assigning victim-perpetrator roles and creating a fair and supportive environment.

CHAPTER 9

ACTIVE COMPANIES
THE POWER OF CULTURE

Sexualized violence in the workplace is unacceptable, and companies must take action—this has been made clear in the previous chapters.

This includes ensuring that those affected do not fear negative reactions, stigmatization, or professional consequences. Observers must also be able to intervene and address the issue publicly without fearing negative repercussions such as exclusion, victim-blaming, or career stagnation.

However, insufficient, unclear, or ineffective procedures still prevent those involved from speaking out.

Therefore, it is our collective responsibility to shape our work environment into safe spaces. Spaces where people are respected, valued, and welcomed, regardless of age, background, language, religion, competence, disability, family status, gender identity, gender, or sexual orientation. This enables everyone to openly address incidents, risks, and concerns.

Every person can contribute to creating a respectful environment in their role and function—whether in dealing with sexualized violence or other conflicts, discrimination, bullying, bossing, or staffing. By acknowledging that sexualized violence is also an issue in our lives, we can actively contribute to a violence-free solution.

Because Safe Work concerns us all.

FROM PREVENTION TO SUPPORT: SAFE WORK

Prevention, intervention, and rehabilitation are crucial steps that companies must take if they want to address inappropriate and violent behaviors in the workplace with determination and sincerity:

1. Prevention
Clear guidelines and procedures, as well as a corporate culture that values and respects diversity, can prevent many incidents before they occur.

2. Information
Processes must be straightforward and transparently accessible to all involved. Confidentiality policies also ensure the protection of individuals' privacy.

3. Training
Regular training and awareness programs provide information on legal and organizational aspects as well as practical guidance and case studies. The goal is to bring everyone in the company to the same level of knowledge, develop a common language, and equip them with the ability to take action.

4. Intervention
Acting quickly and appropriately in the event of an incident is crucial. This includes an immediate investigation, support for the affected person, and, if necessary, disciplinary action against the responsible party. A transparent and fair approach to such situations is important to build trust in the effectiveness of measures and to ensure that such incidents are reported.

5. Investigation
Investigations into allegations of inappropriate behavior are conducted fairly, impartially, objectively, and using the four-eyes principle.

6. Rehabilitation
Counseling services, psychological support, or coaching after an incident and during the investigation help all employees process events and feel safe and comfortable at work again. Rehabilitation and behavioral change programs should also be available for the perpetrator.

Only the combination of these steps enables a comprehensive, long-term, and sustainable shift toward violence-free workplaces and work cultures.

CLEAR GUIDELINES: BINDING CODES OF CONDUCT

A respectful work environment is crucial for both all employees and the company's value creation. Binding codes of conduct and anti-harassment policies play a key role in creating and maintaining this environment:

Clarity, leaving no room for misunderstanding
Policies are clearly and precisely formulated, defining which behaviors are acceptable and which are not tolerated. Depending on the company, it is essential to translate these guidelines into plain language and multiple languages to ensure that everyone can access, understand, and implement them.

Binding for everyone
The policies apply to everyone in the company and to all business partners, regardless of position or hierarchy level. Violations of the policies have consequences, ranging from disciplinary actions to termination.

Easy accessibility for all
The guidelines are easily accessible and available in various inclusive formats—both analog and digital.

Active communication
The guidelines are regularly communicated and reinforced through internal communication channels, visibly placed notices, or discussions in team meetings.

Up-to-date and adaptable
The policies are regularly reviewed, involving all leadership and employees, to keep them current and ensure their effectiveness.

SAFE SPACES:
ARCHITECTURAL PROTECTION

Not only cultural and human factors influence incidents—architectural aspects do as well. Isolated or secluded spaces, dark corners, basements, storage rooms, or deserted areas increase the risk of sexualized violence.

Because often the rule is: Where there are no witnesses, there are no crimes.

Lonely and hard-to-monitor places provide perpetrators with the opportunity to attack individuals. Insufficiently monitored or poorly lit areas allow perpetrators to act undetected and intimidate others through isolation. A lack of access restrictions, unlocked doors, or uncontrolled sensitive areas make it easier for perpetrators to commit crimes in secret. Missing security measures encourage such incidents, as potential perpetrators are not deterred, and those affected are not adequately protected. Narrow spaces without escape routes, as well as unclear or poorly visible areas, pose risk factors for sexualized violence in the workplace. Often, these architectural risks and security deficiencies can be improved with quickly implementable optimizations:

1. Review and Adjustment
Identifying isolated or secluded areas allows for optimized visibility of these zones. Adequate lighting, especially in basements, storage rooms, and other remote areas, reduces potential hazards. Where possible, room design should be open and easily visible. Mirrors, which help eliminate blind spots and are affordable and easy to install, can also make spaces more visible and thus safer.

2. Implementation of Surveillance Systems

Surveillance cameras in strategic locations ensure comprehensive monitoring, provided this is legally permissible and misuse is prevented. Clearly visible signs indicating their presence deter potential perpetrators and contribute to an increased sense of security. They are particularly valuable investments in parking lots and underground garages.

3. Improvement of Access Rights and Controls

Restricting access to sensitive or potentially dangerous areas through locking systems and access cards ensures that only authorized individuals can enter and that doors remain locked when not in use. This significantly reduces the chances of unauthorized access and criminal acts.

4. Escape Routes and Emergency Exits

Clearly visible and easily accessible escape routes in all areas, especially in narrow or secluded spaces, mark exit options from dangerous situations.

5. Regular Security Inspections

Regular reviews of security measures and facilities ensure their effectiveness and functionality while helping to identify new risks. This ensures that protection remains up-to-date at all times.

CHAPTER 10

ACTIVE POLITICS
THE POWER OF LAWS

As outlined in Chapter 7, there are currently numerous laws, guidelines, and programs developed by political systems and ministries to counteract sexualized violence in the workplace.

But how effective are these measures really?

Studies show that despite existing laws and guidelines, many cases of sexualized violence go unreported. This is often due to a lack of trustworthy and independent complaint offices or because past experiences have shown that reports are not sufficiently pursued.

POLITICAL NEED FOR ACTION: MORE THAN JUST LAWS

The review of existing laws reveals that effective sanctions are often missing. Companies that fail to comply with their legal obligations frequently face no negative consequences - a situation that urgently needs to change.

There is an urgent and extensive need for political action to ensure that the power of laws is optimally utilized. The political level must act cohesively and holistically to effectively combat sexualized violence in the workplace, as the current legal framework is insufficient.

Political systems and ministries must therefore develop further-reaching laws and guidelines and ensure their consistent implementation and enforcement. An expansion of the General Equal Treatment Act, as demanded by the Independent Federal Commissioner for Anti-Discrimination in July 2023[54], is also necessary. For example, through:

Solutions for SMEs
Small and medium-sized enterprises (SMEs) have not always established complaint offices despite legal requirements—due to a lack of capacity and overarching solutions. They often lack the resources to create and maintain effective complaint offices. For these companies, inter-company complaint offices should be set up with the support of the relevant chambers.

Stronger Sanctions for Companies
Stronger sanctions for violations of protection regulations already exist. German labor law provides for fines and other legal consequences if companies fail in their duty to prevent and educate about "sexual harassment."

However, there is ongoing debate about whether the existing regulations are sufficient or effective enough. Minimum standards for corporate complaint procedures and clear authorities for complaint offices should be defined in Section 13 of the General Equal Treatment Act. The absence of complaint offices should be considered an indication of potential discrimination, which could lead to claims for damages or compensation.

Mandatory Reporting Obligations

Companies should be required to regularly report on measures and incidents related to sexualized violence. These reports could be published in an anonymized form to create transparency and encourage companies to actively engage with the issue. An annual national report would help identify progress or deficits. Mandatory reporting obligations regarding sexualized violence are not yet widely established. However, some companies voluntarily publish reports on gender equality and diversity.

Explicit Expansion of labor laws to schools and Universities

The General Equal Treatment Act already protects against discrimination and "sexual harassment" in educational institutions, but the regulations are not always specific enough, particularly regarding the practical challenges in schools and universities. While "sexual harassment" by teaching staff and among students is fundamentally prohibited and can be pursued under labor or disciplinary law, enforcing this prohibition is difficult, especially in situations with significant power imbalances, such as during exams or thesis evaluations.

Expansion of Labor Laws to Civil Law

Harassment can also occur in other civil law contractual

relationships, such as rental agreements or memberships, significantly affecting the rights of those affected. There is currently no legal protection in these areas. Therefore, labor laws should be expanded to cover the entire civil law domain to include "sexual harassment" in the context of service provision.

Expansion of the labor laws to Freelancers
Labor laws often only protects employees. Freelancers, workers in external companies, and volunteers are not sufficiently protected. Interns are also not currently included. Therefore, the scope of application in Section 6(1) of the General Equal Treatment Act should be expanded to include these groups, and protection for workers in external companies should be extended to all forms of outsourced personnel.

Expansion of Labor Laws to ADM
The digital transformation is increasingly leading to automated decision-making systems (ADM) in the workplace and business transactions. Algorithms play a central role, for example, in recruitment or salary calculations. Although these systems are often considered objective, they can contain biases and distortions from the data used, leading to inequality and discrimination. Therefore, the use of ADM should be recognized as a potential basis for discrimination.

Easing the Burden of Proof
In legal proceedings, the ability to provide evidence remains a significant challenge. Those affected must first present indications or clues (circumstantial evidence) suggesting harassment. If the court deems these indications sufficient and considers the harassment probable, the burden of proof shifts. The other party must then prove that no harassment occurred. In practice,

however, it is often difficult to determine which indications are sufficient and how they should be weighted. This leads to inconsistent interpretations and rulings. Currently, those affected must fully prove both the discrimination and the circumstantial evidence. Although labor laws provides for an easing of the burden of proof, it is not sufficient. It is often difficult to present the necessary indications without concrete information about the reasons, such as rejection of applicants or discrimination. To improve the enforcement of rights, the requirement for proof should be reduced to a credible demonstration - meaning that a predominant probability should suffice. Laws should define concrete standard examples such as sworn affidavits, testing procedures, or the absence of a complaint office as sufficient indications.

Right to Information
Labor laws should be supplemented with a right to information, allowing those affected to request specific information from the other party that could support their position. This would ease the burden on those affected, as they would not have to rely solely on their own evidence. Additionally, the refusal to provide requested information could be considered an indication of discrimination.

Effective Sanctions
European legal requirements stipulate that sanctions for "sexual harassment" must be effective, proportionate, and dissuasive, particularly regarding the amount of compensation. In practice, however, these compensations often amount to only a low three-digit sum in euros. Additionally, there is a tendency in case law to require a minimum severity of the act to justify compensation. However, such a "triviality threshold" contradicts both the wording and purpose of labor laws. Therefore they all should explicitly state that sanctions for discrimination

must be effective, proportionate, and dissuasive.

Collective Legal Action

Those affected often hesitate to assert their rights due to lengthy legal proceedings, high costs, and associated risks. Additionally, the unclear case law in anti-discrimination law makes it difficult to assess the chances of success of a lawsuit, leading to a lack of effective discrimination protection. A right to collective legal action and the possibility of third-party representation could counteract this. Collective legal action allows specific organizations or associations to file lawsuits on behalf of their members or the general public. This means these organizations can assert rights or claims without individual affected persons having to sue themselves. Third-party representation allows a person or institution to file a lawsuit in their own name but in the interest of others. This means someone can act in a legal dispute to enforce the rights of another person who may not be able to do so themselves.

A right to collective legal action would enable qualified anti-discrimination organizations to take legal action in cases of structural discrimination without individual involvement and thus establish fundamental case law that provides legal certainty for affected individuals in their own lawsuits. Third-party representation would allow organizations to assert individual rights for those affected, thereby relieving them of the burden.By introducing collective legal action and third-party representation, associations, trade unions, and anti-discrimination organizations could file lawsuits on behalf of those affected, strengthening collective legal protection and helping individuals enforce their rights without having to stand alone against powerful employers or institutions.

Strengthening Works Councils and Trade Unions

Works councils and trade unions should be strengthened as they play a crucial role in protecting workers' rights and enforcing anti-discrimination measures in the workplace.

FACTS AS A WEAPON:
THE POWER OF DATA AND RESEARCH

Research and data are crucial tools in the fight against sexualized violence in the workplace. It is essential to have up-to-date and gender-inclusive data and statistics to understand the scope of the problem, identify trends, and make informed policy decisions.

Through research, we gain important insights that serve as a foundation for developing effective prevention strategies, intervention measures, and awareness campaigns. Current data allow for a better understanding of the dynamics of sexualized violence in the workplace—by identifying affected industries, perpetrator profiles, the impact on victims and the work environment, as well as indirect consequences. Gender-inclusive data and statistics provide a comprehensive view of the diverse experiences and challenges associated with sexualized violence in the workplace. This includes considering different gender identities and sexual orientations to develop targeted and inclusive measures that address the needs of all affected individuals.

Therefore, political support for research and access to comprehensive data are essential to enable a well-founded approach to combating sexualized violence in the workplace. Resources must be allocated, and measures taken to actively support researchers in this field, improve data collection and analysis, and ensure the availability of up-to-date data.

CHAPTER 11

ACTIVE SOCIETY
THE POWER OF MANY

The #MeToo movement has heightened global awareness of sexualized violence and harassment.

People have been, and continue to be, encouraged to share their experiences, bringing the urgency of addressing this issue to the forefront.

This increased visibility has helped challenge societal norms and break down stereotypes. Because we are many.

#METOO:
YOU TOO?

In October 2017, actress Alyssa Milano used the hashtag #MeToo, urging women to share their experiences with sexualized violence. This simple yet powerful call was taken up by millions of people worldwide and quickly spread across social media. The viral nature of the campaign enabled personal stories and experiences to reach a massive audience. By sharing their experiences, many others felt empowered to tell their own stories. This solidarity created a supportive community where survivors could share their experiences in a safe space.

The media picked up the topic, reporting extensively on survivors' stories and the systemic issues involved. Reports about high-profile figures accused of sexual misconduct brought the discussions into the mainstream and heightened public awareness.

#MeToo has played a crucial role in ensuring that sexualized violence is no longer viewed as a private or marginal issue. #MeToo has changed attitudes. #MeToo has given survivors a voice, won public support, and helped break stigmas. In many countries and organizations, legal and policy reforms have been initiated to address sexualized violence and its prevention.

The #MeToo movement has demonstrated that, through the powerful combination of public pressure, media coverage, and individual courage, taboos can be broken, and we can collectively rethink and act differently—even though we are not yet at the end of the journey that #MeToo has set in motion.

NEW STANDARDS:
THE SOCIETAL CODE OF CONDUCT

We need a shared Code of Conduct that places non-violence, equality, and diversity at its core. This Code of Conduct consists of common values, norms, and rules that must be respected. Everyone can contribute within their own environment by taking responsibility and ensuring that violence is not tolerated. This can mean being attentive, speaking up about suspicious situations, offering support to those affected, or actively standing against discrimination and harassment.

Everyone can make a difference.
This also includes showing civil courage—always, of course, without putting oneself or others in danger. Because if we do not actively stand against discrimination and violence or fail to seek help in specific situations, we create space for further abuse and increasingly dangerous actions. We can stand up for each other more—both in small ways and in significant actions. Often, we have a gut feeling about when and how we should intervene.

Not looking away but PAYING ATTENTION.

Not ignoring but LISTENING.

Not remaining silent but RAISING OUR VOICES.

Every time we take a stand and seek help, we demonstrate civil courage. Of course, civil courage also means stepping out of our comfort zone, possibly entering uncomfortable situations, intervening unprompted, and voicing our opinions.

Those who show civil courage often accept disadvantages, risks, and dangers to stand up for others and offer selfless help. Yet, a democratic society cannot exist without courage driven by human and democratic principles.

And what many do not know: Everyone is legally obliged to help within their individual capabilities. If we fail to assist a person in distress, we may be liable for failure to render aid. Likewise, laws allows us to defend ourselves and others in an emergency without acting unlawfully. This includes not putting ourselves in unnecessary danger.

But what we can always do is seek help—by calling the police, asking others for support, or reaching out to security personnel, responsible authorities, or expert organizations.

CONNECTING OR DIVIDING:
THE ROLE OF THE MEDIA

The media plays a central role in reporting on sexualized violence. The way and extent to which they cover such cases—whether in companies, everyday life, or society at large—has a significant impact on how we all deal with this issue. The media both reflect and shape how survivors are perceived and treated and what solutions we pursue.

A positive example of media influence is well-researched reporting on successful prevention, intervention, and support measures. Newspapers, magazines, radio and television programs, and podcasts that highlight effective approaches help raise awareness of sexualized violence and promote positive change. Documentaries and investigative films that provide in-depth insights also offer valuable education.

However, media also bear great responsibility in how they report. Sensationalist coverage and the use of sexism or gender stereotypes for entertainment purposes are not just problematic—they are dangerous. Respectful and inclusive reporting is essential to strengthening survivors' perspectives and driving societal change.

Entertainment Sexism for Clicks?

Particularly concerning are problematic portrayals of sexualized violence in reality TV shows. These formats often feature sexist comments, gender stereotypes, discriminatory attitudes, and boundary violations.

Whether in dating shows, talent competitions, or challenge-based formats - such scenes are not only shocking but also dangerous. They reinforce and normalize discriminatory and harmful attitudes, especially for young and impressionable audiences. Research has shown that exposure to offensive or sexualized portrayals of gender roles in media increases tolerance for sexualized violence - a deeply concerning phenomenon.

But it's not just reality TV. Films, magazines, and podcasts also spread problematic depictions and content, promoting unhealthy attitudes and behaviors. The spread of sexist and inappropriate content leads to imitation effects and can ultimately result in real violence. It is therefore crucial that media outlets critically examine the content they distribute. Thoughtful and respectful reporting has a positive impact and ensures that sexualized violence is addressed appropriately - turning it into a collective issue that we must tackle together.

UNITED IN ACTION: GOAL-ORIENTED COLLABORATIONS

Ending sexualized violence requires, as the previous chapters have shown, coordinated and joint approaches. An isolated approach is not enough to find effective solutions.

This is where the collaboration of various stakeholders comes into play: businesses, trade unions, victim organizations, civil society organizations, NGOs (Non-Governmental Organizations), companies, educational institutions, kindergartens, associations, sports facilities, and all other relevant entities can work together. Studies show that goal-oriented collaboration is crucial for achieving sustainable change. A 2014 study by the European Institute for Gender Equality (EIGE)[55] emphasizes that coordinated cooperation across societal, political, and individual levels is necessary.

An example of a successful partnership is the collaboration between an NGO, an educational institution, and a company:

An NGO
brings expertise and experience in handling sexualized violence.

An educational institution
provides a platform for awareness-raising.

A company
provides financial resources for prevention programs.

Through these pooled resources and expertise, more effective strategies are developed and implemented. The foundation of

a successful partnership lies in trust, respect, and shared goals. Open and transparent communication is essential to overcoming obstacles and finding solutions together.
It is important to consider different perspectives and take the needs and rights of those involved seriously. The voices of survivors must be heard in order to develop effective and compassionate solutions.

Committed partnerships have the potential to raise awareness in society and change social norms. Through joint public relations efforts, campaigns, and educational initiatives, the issue of sexualized violence is brought into greater public focus. The World Health Organization (WHO) also repeatedly emphasizes in its publications the importance of awareness campaigns and educational initiatives in increasing awareness of sexualized violence and changing the culture of tolerance.

Political support for such collaborations strengthens collective efforts to exchange best practices and pool resources, thereby enabling the implementation of effective measures.

The importance of cooperation and coordination cannot be overstated!

FROM VICTIMS TO SURVIVORS: WHAT WORDS CAN DO

The way we talk and think about sexualized violence in the workplace has profound effects. The shift from the term "victim" to "survivor" and the associated change in attitude are, for example, crucial for supporting and empowering those affected.

Words are more than just a string of letters.

They shape our perception and influence the self-understanding of the individuals affected.

Victim

The term "victim" evokes unwanted associations of weakness, helplessness, and powerlessness. This label can amplify the feeling that the affected person is permanently inferior or defined by the trauma they have experienced.

Survivor

In contrast, the term "survivor" carries a positive connotation of resilience, strength, and self-empowerment. It acknowledges that the affected person is not only a victim of circumstances but also plays an active role in their own healing process. The transformation from "victim" to "survivor" encourages viewing those affected as resilient and capable, promoting control over their story.

Attitude

Attitude is a path to healing. A respectful and supportive attitude recognizes the severity of the experiences and respects the personal integrity of the individual. It creates a protected environment. A respectful attitude promotes healing processes and positively influences the overall work climate. A culture of appreciation and understanding increases the willingness to address incidents openly and find solutions.

Self-Efficacy

By changing the language and the way we talk about sexualized violence, we make an important contribution to broader societal change and become effective ourselves. We send the signal that we take sexualized violence seriously and see the affected individuals as strong and capable. This strengthens a shift in thinking within society and reduces stigmatization, prejudices, and inappropriate reactions.

Furthermore, the way we speak and think influences changes that are crucial for developing strategies that ultimately benefit everyone.

TRUE EQUALITY:
THE COLLECTIVE PATH

True equality is inseparably linked to the strategy for eliminating sexualized violence. The path toward it requires a joint effort from society, institutions, communities, and individuals to bring about structural change and raise collective awareness. This journey necessitates the cooperation of all genders. True equality means that all people—regardless of gender or gender identity—have the same rights, opportunities, and possibilities. Each of us can contribute by questioning gender images and roles and promoting equal opportunities for all.

Men, in particular, are now more than ever called upon to actively and in a feminist way promote equality and take a stand against sexualized violence. While women have long been doing this in many areas, men often feel overwhelmed or uncertain about their role in feminism. However, feminism is not just about advocating for women's rights. The goal is not to replace men in power with women. Rather, many feminist approaches aim to achieve a fair distribution of power and resources, as well as greater self-determination for all genders. It is about creating structures that enable every person to live their life free from discrimination and violence. Yet, not everyone shares this view.

This becomes particularly evident in discussions surrounding #NotAllMen.

#NOTALLMEN:
YET TOO MANY

The hashtag #NotAllMen emerged in response to the increasing visibility of discussions on gender-based and sexualized violence, particularly violence by men against women. The phrase became popular in early 2000s social media and is used to emphasize that not all men commit acts of sexualized violence. Some men use the hashtag to distance themselves from these accusations and highlight that they are not part of the problem. But it's not that simple.

The hashtag is controversial because it often distracts from the actual issue. Critics argue that the discussion about gender-based violence does not accuse all men but rather highlights the systemic problems that enable such violence. When men use #NotAllMen to defend themselves, it diverts attention from the experiences of survivors and from finding collective solutions to the problem.

The fact is: worldwide women experience significantly more physical harassment than men. In both cases, perpetrators are most often men. Men pose a potential threat to women. Women cannot know which man might be dangerous and which might not. As a result, women assess men as either trustworthy or potentially dangerous based on their past experiences. Men in family or professional environments are often given the benefit of the doubt, which simultaneously makes it harder to identify and confront actual perpetrators.

But what about men who are strangers or random encounters? Men who walk behind women at night, share an elevator, or cross paths at an event?
We all know that not all men are sexist, commit sexual assaults, or are born as sexual offenders. Yet, almost all women experience some form of sexualized violence at some point in

their lives - whether in the form of sexism, misogyny, or actual physical assault - at home, on the street, or in the workplace. These experiences shape women's daily lives.

Uncertainty leads to avoidance.

This uncertainty causes many women to feel fear and discomfort, as they cannot discern men's intentions. It is a constant balancing act between hoping that the other person poses no threat and being cautious enough to ensure their own safety. Many women report automatically taking precautionary measures in such situations: keeping their keys ready, switching to the other side of the street, avoiding eye contact, or pretending to be on the phone.

Another consequence of this uncertainty - of not knowing who might be dangerous - is that women, and of course, other individuals affected by sexualized violence, integrate avoidance strategies into their daily lives. Many adjust their behavior to protect themselves from potential dangers. They wear loose clothing, avoid being alone at night, prefer female taxi drivers, use apps for safe routes home, and agree on emergency signals with friends. These precautions limit their lives, personal expression, and behavior.

Men, on the other hand, benefit in many ways from patriarchal and sexist structures. They often have better job prospects and are paid more for the same work than women. Men are also less likely to experience sexualized violence in the workplace.

Using the hashtag #NotAllMen can thus be seen as a refusal to acknowledge the structural violence that women worldwide suffer from. Instead of feeling personally attacked by such discussions, men should take the opportunity to recognize these issues and understand that conversations about experiences of violence are meant to raise awareness and drive positive change—not to demonize all men.

To help women feel safer in everyday situations and at work, men can consciously adjust their behavior and be mindful of how their actions are perceived. In public spaces, men can cross the street or increase distance to avoid making a woman feel followed. They can be aware of their body language and tone of voice to avoid unintentionally appearing threatening. They can consciously act respectfully and respect boundaries, especially in situations where women may feel vulnerable— such as in public transport or confined spaces.

At work, men can reflect on their privileges and actively support women's career development by offering mentorship or advocating for equality within their company. They can be mindful and ensure they are respectful and supportive colleagues. This includes maintaining physical distance, avoiding unnecessary closeness, and ensuring that women are heard in meetings and discussions. Men can also intervene when they witness sexist remarks or behavior. Small gestures like these already make a significant difference in women's sense of security. They are part of a broader effort and are essential.

#TooManyMen & #YesAllWomen

To support these efforts and raise awareness of the issue, the hashtag #TooManyMen has recently gained traction. Women use this hashtag to share their experiences and highlight how difficult it is to feel safe in a male-dominated world. They emphasize that it is not about generalizing all men but rather about pointing out the countless situations in which too many men are still perceived as threats or behave in a consciously or unconsciously intimidating way. Men are called upon to actively participate in this change by reflecting on their role, raising awareness, and standing in solidarity with those affected.

Similarly, the hashtag #YesAllWomen has emerged, under which women share their frequent experiences with harassment, discrimination, and sexual violence to shed light on the reality of women's lives. The vast number of these reports shows that these are not isolated incidents but rather a deeply rooted, systemic problem.

Both hashtags underscore the urgent need for comprehensive societal and structural change in how we coexist.

STOP

IT

CHAPTER 12

COMPETENCES
FOR SAFE SUPPORT

Sexualized violence in the workplace affects not only the individuals directly involved but also the designated contact persons who are supposed to support them.

These contact persons often face immense pressure, as they must remain neutral while supporting those affected, and at the same time, they may need to investigate colleagues and take actions that the company might not necessarily welcome.

And that is challenging.

FROM ZERO TO HERO:
CONFIDENT CONTACT PERSONS

Not all contact persons have taken on their role voluntarily. This makes it even more demanding to meet the associated challenges. They must detach themselves from hierarchies and loyalties and develop the necessary competencies.

Empathy and sensitivity toward the experiences and emotions of those affected are essential to interact with them respectfully and with understanding. It is important to remember that contact persons are usually neither legal nor therapeutic experts and should refer those affected to appropriate professionals or resources when necessary.

At the same time, they must ensure that all information is handled confidentially and processed in compliance with data protection regulations—unless there are legal or ethical obligations to disclose certain information. Neutrality and impartiality are crucial, enabling contact persons to handle situations objectively and encourage affected individuals to make their own decisions without pressure.

Beyond empathetic communication, expertise and competence in dealing with sexualized violence are required. Contact persons should be familiar with relevant laws, policies, and procedures to provide appropriate guidance. Ensuring safety and protection throughout the process is essential—by providing information about support services, securing evidence, or implementing protective measures. Additionally, ongoing support beyond the initial contact must be ensured so that affected individuals continue to have access to appropriate assistance and resources.

Cultural sensitivity is also crucial to respect different backgrounds, values, and concerns. Clear and understandable communication informs individuals about the process, available options, and relevant resources. Contact persons should continuously refine their skills through targeted training and regular reflection.

By engaging with experienced colleagues or mentors, they can learn from practical experiences. Seeking feedback from conversation partners and consistently evaluating and adjusting their communication style strengthens their professional and interpersonal skills, allowing them to fulfill their role with confidence. The following field-tested methods and communication strategies provide valuable support in this regard.

THE ACTION© METHOD:
FOR EMPATHETIC RESPONSES

ACTION©, developed by the act & protect® Academy, serves as an initial approach to support contact persons in handling communication during specific situations. Through comprehensive competency development, contact persons become true and confident heroes. They play a vital role in addressing sexualized violence.

The ACTION© method provides a practical guide for leaders and contact persons to act empathetically and confidently in challenging and emotional conversations. Active listening, clear communication, and sharing available support options help establish a safe and supportive environment. Implementing courage, organizing resources, and following up on progress are key steps in building long-term support and trust.

This method fosters trust and ensures that affected individuals receive the necessary assistance and feel protected in their work environment. Ideally, such conversations should take place in a quiet, private space, free from unwanted observers or eavesdroppers.

Why Is This Important?

Holding the conversation in a protected space is essential to maintaining trust and enabling open communication. It safeguards privacy and ensures that sensitive information does not inadvertently reach third parties. This promotes the integrity of the conversation and creates a secure and trustworthy environment. Key Aspects for Initial Conversations

Discretion

Ensure that there are no interruptions or disturbances during the conversation. The affected person should have enough time to describe the incident in detail. Start with only a few questions and minimize interruptions. Before taking notes, obtain consent and explain why note-taking is necessary.

Confidentiality

Address confidentiality: How will the complaint be handled, and who must be informed? Clearly define your role and responsibilities. Ensure that all information is treated confidentially and accessible only to authorized individuals. Use secure network environments and solutions.

Empathy and Sensitivity

Show empathy towards the individuals involved and acknowledge their concerns. Demonstrate that the incident is being taken seriously. Arrange a follow-up meeting to discuss further steps or outcomes.

Be transparent about the next steps:
What information will be shared with the accused? What actions are possible and planned? How will the process continue?

Only commit to measures that can be implemented. Inform affected individuals about external support options, such as counseling services, family and close contacts, doctors, and therapists. After the conversation, proceed with all procedural steps only in consultation with the affected person. Ensure they are informed before the accused is confronted with the allegations. If third parties need to be involved, obtain the affected person's consent. Confrontations between the involved parties are not a suitable measure and should be strictly avoided.

Documentation

Record key points from the conversation to gather all relevant information while complying with data protection regulations. Document the incident as precisely as possible. Explain your questions and follow-ups to maintain transparency and avoid misunderstandings or the impression of an interrogation. Clearly state that detailed witness accounts or memory logs are crucial.

Objectivity

Maintain a neutral stance throughout the process. Avoid interpreting or evaluating statements—document them objectively. Refrain from incorporating personal opinions or emotions to ensure fair and unbiased handling of the case.

A structured approach builds trust and confidence and lays the foundation for constructive and respectful communication throughout the process.

A First Conversation Using ACTION©

Introduction
> "Thank you for trusting me with this. I want to ensure we can speak in a safe and confidential setting. Is that okay for you?"

A - ctive and Open Listening
> "It's good that you are bringing this up."
> "I can understand that..."
> "I am here to listen to you and support you."

C - lear Communication
> "First, I want to make it clear that sexualized violence is absolutely unacceptable to me."
> "I take your concerns very seriously, and I am here to support you by..."
> "I will follow our internal guidelines, which means..."

T - alking About Support Options
> "The following support options are available..."
> "I am happy to help you get in touch."
> "I will send you an email with the contact details."

I - nstilling Courage
> "You have already taken an important step!"
> "It takes a lot of courage to do this."
> "The company will do everything possible to find a good solution."

O - rganizing and Activating Resources
> "I will immediately take the necessary steps..."
> "You can reach out to this person for support..."
> "Please do not hesitate to contact me."

N - ext Steps

"We will meet regularly to ensure you receive the necessary support."
"Would it be okay if I check in with you again next week?""

Conclusion

"Thank you for speaking with me. We will work together to ensure that you feel safe and receive the support you need."

Depending on internal guidelines, the individuals involved, and the company culture, such conversations can be adapted accordingly.

Practice this.
In your thoughts, with colleagues, and with supervisors. The more confident you are in handling these conversations, the more security and trust you can offer to those affected.

CONVERSATIONS WITH ACCUSED PERSONS: CLARIFICATION

Accused individuals have the right to an objective and factual investigation process. The legal assessment and choice of measures depend on the specific circumstances of each individual case. Employers, contact persons, process participants, and leadership figures must therefore act with care and responsibility to ensure the protection of the affected person while also safeguarding the rights of the accused individual and protecting them from workplace gossip, defamation, and bullying.

In urgent cases, it is essential for all responsible parties to act immediately to stop any harm caused by the accused person. At the same time, it is important to fully clarify the facts to make an informed decision. The evaluation of "sexual harassment" always depends on the individual case. The determination of whether an incident has occurred is made independently of the context, work environment, or situation. The key question is: Did the sexual harassment occur or not?

A personnel meeting with the accused person is necessary—both to provide them with a transparent opportunity to respond to the allegations and to obtain a comprehensive account of the incident. The accused person should be given the chance to present their perspective. Throughout the conversation, neutrality must be the top priority. If the accused denies the allegations, those responsible for the investigation must assess the credibility of their statements.

Observing the accused person's reactions during the conversation can be helpful.

Surprise

Is the accused person surprised by the allegations? A genuine reaction of surprise can indicate that the person was unaware of the accusations. However, an exaggerated display of shock might suggest a staged response.

Seriousness

Does the accused person take the allegations seriously, or do they try to downplay the situation? A serious and reflective reaction indicates that the accused understands the gravity of the situation. Conversely, trivializing the allegations may suggest an unwillingness to take responsibility for their behavior.

Awareness

Is the accused person familiar with the described incident? How do they react to it? Are they aware of the problem? Do they respond with justification, minimization, or shifting blame? A reaction that aims to shift blame onto others can signal a defensive stance and a denial of personal responsibility.

After the conversation, it is crucial to carefully document the accused person's reactions and statements. If they admit to the misconduct, appropriate sanctions must be implemented immediately.

If the allegations are otherwise confirmed, suitable measures must be taken. Depending on the case, these may range from preventive actions to formal warnings or even dismissal. Employers have some discretion, but this is significantly reduced in cases of serious violations. It is the responsibility of leadership to carefully assess the severity and provability of the incident and determine appropriate measures. Factors such as repeat offenses, remorse expressed by the accused, and the overall context of the incident play a key role in this decision.

If the accused person persistently denies the allegations, the situation can become complex. In such cases, it may be beneficial to involve external professionals, such as conflict counselors, women's and violence support services, or legal and psychological advisors.

Additionally, after the conversation, it is important to inform the affected person that the meeting has taken place— without disclosing confidential details.

EMPOWERMENT:
INSTEAD OF HELPLESSNESS

Every company should offer all employees—regardless of their position or length of service—the opportunity or even the obligation to continue developing their skills in sensitivity, self-efficacy, communication, and behavior. Companies have a tremendous opportunity to take a clear stance, which has a lasting positive impact.

Now is the time for both individuals and groups to recognize their own thought and behavior patterns and to question and change stereotypical and sexualized aspects of how we think, speak, and act. The goal is to break down biases, critically examine everyday attitudes, create a culture of appreciation and inclusion, and implement a shared Code of Conduct.

Regular training sessions for all employees, including leadership and new hires, should be a given. Providing everyone with the necessary tools and resources is essential. Beyond that, fostering an open communication culture where people feel safe sharing experiences and receiving support is crucial.

By focusing on empowerment instead of helplessness, companies actively contribute to positive workplace change and create a corporate culture in which everyone becomes a multiplier for progress.

ZERO TOLERANCE, FULL IMPACT: LEADERSHIP AS A ROLEMODEL

Creating a culture of respect is an exciting journey—often requiring a paradigm shift. Instead of helplessness and ignorance, empowerment is needed - affecting all members of a company as a large, interdependent team.

Companies must do more than make empty promises or display symbolic gestures at scheduled times. Real change requires courage and commitment, even if it means stepping out of the comfort zone. But the benefits for both companies and individuals are enormous!

Leadership plays a decisive role. Leaders are role models, bear responsibility, and serve as multipliers and change agents. By sending clear messages and making it evident that sexualized violence is unacceptable and will have consequences, they not only strengthen their own position but also shape workplace culture.

Leaders must be familiar with and enforce established guidelines and procedures for the prevention and intervention of sexual harassment. This means:

Taking a clear stance

As a leader, it is crucial to clearly define what constitutes sexual harassment and make it unmistakably clear that it will not be tolerated within the team. Communicate that such behavior leads to professional and legal consequences. Reject any attempt to dismiss these incidents as jokes or misunderstandings—this strengthens both your leadership role and workplace safety.

Destigmatizing the topic
Talk openly about sexual harassment—not just when an incident occurs. Make it clear that you are available as a point of contact and, if possible, designate additional contact persons of different genders.

Shaping team culture
Create a work environment that prevents misconduct by identifying potential risk factors such as infrastructure, working hours, or team dynamics. Actively oppose abuses of power and toxic competition while fostering a respectful workplace culture. If you witness sexual harassment, intervene immediately and take reports from affected individuals or third parties seriously. Ensure proper documentation and confidentiality.

Seeking expertise
Use internal policies, legal frameworks, and expert advice to prevent sexual harassment. Consult professional support services when necessary.

Fulfilling the duty of care
Actively offer support and inform affected individuals about available resources. Coordinate protective measures to prevent further harm. Ensure that the accused and the affected person do not have to interact in the workplace. Protect accused individuals from premature judgments. Be transparent about the steps being taken, particularly regarding inquiries, documentation, and follow-up actions. If a criminal offense has occurred, inform the affected person about the option of filing a police report and direct them to appropriate legal and counseling services.

Taking responsibility
Diligently document every complaint, review it carefully,

and inform the affected individual about the results. Ensure that the complaint process does not lead to disadvantages for the affected person. Avoid direct confrontation between the accused and the complainant, but objectively hear out both sides. If necessary, impose appropriate sanctions or take measures for rehabilitation.

And always remember:

Only zero tolerance leads to full impact.

SAFETY FIRST:
PROTECTION CONCEPTS FOR SECURITY

To effectively combat and prevent sexualized violence in the workplace, comprehensive protection strategies are essential. These serve as a reliable framework for all employees and partners, ensuring a safe work environment where individuals can focus on their tasks without fear of harassment.

Tailored protection concepts create barriers for potential offenders while allowing affected individuals to report incidents in a safe and trusted manner. Instead of fostering general suspicion or mistrust, these strategies promote transparency and mutual respect. Employees, as potential stakeholders, play a crucial role in identifying risks and helping develop effective protective measures.

Developing and implementing these protection concepts requires a thorough risk analysis to identify workplace vulnerabilities. This process examines the conditions that could be exploited by perpetrators and explores how existing structures can be adapted for prevention. Engaging with specialized consulting services is highly beneficial in this process.

Investment in protection concepts is a clear indicator of a zero-tolerance approach toward sexualized violence—ensuring safety, respect, and well-being for all employees.

Because nothing is more important than safety first!

CHAPTER 13

CONCRETE AND PRACTICAL TIPS AND METHODS

Unfortunately, there is no universal solution to sexualized violence. Even though we might wish for a magic potion, the problem is too complex and far-reaching to be solved with a simple fix.

It depends on many factors, such as the type of violence, the individuals involved, the context, and the applicable legal regulations.

Reactions to sexualized violence also vary depending on personality and situation, as every person involved and every situation is unique.

SETTING BOUNDARIES: WHAT YOU CAN DO

This chapter discusses possible actions for dealing with sexualized violence. It does not address physical assaults such as rape or attempted sexual violence, as these severe offenses require specific and often immediate responses, which are detailed in other professional literature and resources.

Our focus is on appropriate responses to non-physical forms of sexualized violence, such as verbal and nonverbal boundary violations through language, facial expressions, gestures, and intrusive behavior. These forms of violence are also harmful and distressing and require specific reactions and coping strategies.

People who perceive sexist jokes or sexual remarks as inappropriate are not overly sensitive or humorless. Rather, this reflects a strong sense of self-awareness, a keen perception of others, high emotional intelligence, and a clear understanding of personal boundaries. These abilities are valuable and deserve protection, even if others may perceive the situation differently.

In this context, one thing is essential: Take your feelings and reactions seriously. It is crucial to stand up against any form of boundary violation and to protect your personal limits. As you continue reading, you will find practical tips and guidance on how to maintain and strengthen your boundaries to protect yourself from verbal and nonverbal assaults. Your perception and your boundaries are valid and deserve respect and defense. Additionally, we will introduce assertiveness strategies to help you feel safer and more confident in challenging situations. These methods support your personal integrity.

You Are Not to Blame!

Remember: You are not to blame! It is essential to understand that no one is ever responsible for experiencing sexualized violence. The responsibility always lies with the perpetrator. Blame or self-reproach has no place with those affected.

Take Your Feelings Seriously!

It is normal for those affected by sexualized violence to experience a range of emotions, such as fear, anger, shame, or helplessness. These feelings are valid and should be acknowledged and expressed.

It Is Your Right to Say No or Yes!

Defending your boundaries is the right thing to do, and it is crucial that this is respected. If you do not welcome certain behavior, communicate this clearly. This sends a strong message—to the perpetrator and to yourself. How to do this is explained in the following pages.

Reacting in situations of harassment or violence is not always easy.

Quite the opposite! Most of the time, it is incredibly difficult. And sometimes, we may not understand other people's reactions or lack thereof. However, every person has their own boundaries and comfort zones, where they can act safely and confidently.

Some people prefer verbal responses, while others send nonverbal signals. Others are strong in paraverbal or written communication. Verbal communication refers to spoken and written words, as well as sign language. Nonverbal communication includes posture, movement, gestures, facial expressions, touch, and spatial distance. Paraverbal communication includes all vocal elements accompanying speech, such as volume, pitch, speed, and emphasis.

However, it can still be difficult to react immediately and openly. Fear of consequences, insecurity, or shock often cause paralysis and prevent immediate boundary-setting.
The so-called "Fight, Flight, or Freeze" describes automatic, instinctive reactions of the body to perceived threats or stressful situations:
We either fight (Fight), try to escape the danger by fleeing (Flight), or freeze and become unable to react (Freeze).

These reactions are deeply embedded in the human nervous system and serve survival. They are not to be judged but should be recognized as individual responses.

Additionally, everyone has the right to choose their own way of dealing with such situations—depending on their personal boundaries and comfort zones. However, it is important that you react - even if it is through conscious ignorance. Silence or entirely passive behavior is interpreted by perpetrators as approval.

This leads them to push boundaries further and commit additional transgressions. A confrontation through a personal conversation, a face-to-face meeting, a phone call, or in writing is therefore necessary:

The Personal Conversation

A personal conversation offers the opportunity to express oneself clearly and directly while also utilizing the impact of nonverbal communication. Direct interaction helps prevent misunderstandings and ensures the message is conveyed effectively. It allows for immediate feedback, questions, and clarification of uncertainties.

The Phone Call

Even in a phone call, clear boundaries can be set. Phone calls are a good alternative to personal conversations. Through your voice, you can express your emotions and positions clearly.

The Written Communication

Sometimes, it is difficult for us to speak to the person directly. In such cases, written communication is a suitable alternative. It allows thoughts and feelings to be carefully formulated and responses to be given at one's own pace. Additionally, written records make communication more traceable.

PIW© METHOD:
EFFECTIVE FEEDBACK

The PIW© Method of the act & protect® Academy, inspired by nonviolent communication, provides a guide for how to formulate our response. It is a structured, clear, and respectful method for giving feedback in sensitive or challenging situations, such as hearing a sexist joke, witnessing a boundary violation, or observing other forms of inappropriate behavior.

PIW© aims to create a clear and respectful communication structure that allows for the expression of feelings and concerns without judging the other person. This fosters open and respectful conversations that are constructive for all involved. The PIW© Method consists of three consecutive steps:

1. P - erception

2. I - mpact

3. W - ish

PIW© can be applied in personal conversations, phone calls, or written communications—whether as the affected person, as an observer, or in a leadership role.

1. Perception – Objective and Specific

In this step, you describe the observed action or statement precisely, without adding personal interpretations or judgments. This objective presentation allows the recipient to clearly understand which specific situation or behavior the feedback refers to. It creates a clear foundation for the conversation and helps prevent misunderstandings.

2. Impact – Subjective and Authentic

Next, you describe the subjective impact of the behavior on you personally. By openly expressing the emotional effects of the behavior, the significance of the situation becomes clear. This promotes understanding of individual feelings and reactions and enables more sensitive communication.

3. Wish – Constructive and Specific

In the final step, you express a concrete wish or suggestion for change. These proposals are based on previous observations and subjective reactions and aim to foster positive change. The goal is to provide the recipient with practical and actionable options that contribute to resolving the issue.

PIW© is a valuable tool for setting and defending personal boundaries clearly and respectfully. It helps to avoid misunderstandings and contributes to creating an open, supportive, and productive environment.

PIW© in a concrete situation:

Rahel is sitting with her colleagues in the cafeteria during lunch break. In a lively atmosphere, they are discussing an upcoming project when her colleague Ahmed suddenly makes an inappropriate joke that makes her feel uncomfortable.

Rahel decides to address Ahmed directly. She clearly and precisely formulates her perception without making accusations or judgments:
"Ahmed, when you made that joke just now, I noticed that you said..." (Perception)

She then describes her subjective reaction and how his words affected her:
"For me personally, that felt uncomfortable and unsettled me in that moment." (Impact)

Finally, Rahel expresses what she wishes for the future:
"I would like us to communicate with respect and appreciation in our conversations and to focus on discussing the project or other topics that are enjoyable for all of us." (Wish)

Perhaps this example feels too formal. It can also be expressed more simply:

"Ahmed, what you just said really upset me as a woman. I would like you to avoid such jokes in the future."

The key is to find your own words and language for an appropriate and authentic response.

What matters most is that you respond.

By combining objective observations, subjective reactions, and concrete improvement suggestions, the PIW© Method supports you in strengthening your self-efficacy. It helps to avoid misunderstandings and ensures that you do not make yourself vulnerable or appear overly sensitive, hysterical, or exaggerated. You demonstrate a clear stance—without criminalizing—remaining factual, helpful, relationship-preserving, and confident.

Additionally, it helps distinguish between individuals who unintentionally behave inappropriately and are willing to accept feedback and change their behavior, and those who act strategically. It also enables the identification of systematically acting perpetrators.

THE JOHARI-WINDOW: FROM UNCONSCIOUS TO CONSCIOUS

The PIW© method illuminates unconscious perception gaps. The term "illuminating blind spots" is an established concept in professional literature and practice. However, as authors, we understand and acknowledge that using the phrase "illuminating blind spots" can be discriminatory, particularly toward visually impaired individuals. Therefore, in our book, we use the alternative term "unconscious perception gaps." We also welcome the development and establishment of a more neutral alternative term in professional literature and practice to promote inclusive and respectful language. By providing feedback with PIW© you can help close unconscious perception gaps in others. Or you may be made aware of your own perception gaps by others.

Closing these unconscious perception gaps means becoming aware of our own unconscious biases, beliefs, or behaviors that we would otherwise not recognize. These unconscious areas, known under the aforementioned term "blind spots," are aspects of our personality or behavior that remain hidden from us but are perceived by others. They are often the cause of misunderstandings, conflicts, or inappropriate behavior

Max is a team leader and believes that he fosters a fair and supportive work environment. However, Max tends to consider the opinions of his male colleagues more frequently in meetings and enthusiastically support their ideas, while often overlooking or not addressing the contributions of his female employees. Max is unaware of this behavior. He believes he treats all employees equally and assesses their performance objectively. From his perspective, he is fair and neutral. However, his employees notice this difference.

Max can only become aware of this unconscious perception gap if he is explicitly made aware of it—through a feedback conversation using the PIW© method, an anonymous internal survey, or by reflecting on his own behavior in meetings. Once Max recognizes this, he can actively work toward ensuring equal treatment within his team, for example, by consciously acknowledging and valuing contributions equally.

We all have unconscious perception gaps. Take this book, for example. As authors, we know that we wrote it. We know what content we included and the writing style we chose. However, what we do not know is how you, as a reader, perceive the book. That is our perception gap.

The model behind the concept of unconscious perception gaps is the Johari Window, a model for self-awareness and self-perception that is divided into four areas:

Open Area

This includes everything that is known to both ourselves and others - either because we have shared it or because it is visible. It includes behaviors and attitudes that are perceived by others.

Hidden Area

This area consists of information about ourselves that we are aware of but keep hidden from others. These may be personal thoughts, feelings, or experiences that we choose not to share.

Unknown Area

These aspects of our personality or abilities are unknown to anyone, either because they are unconscious or have not yet emerged in a situation.

Unconscious Perception Gaps

These gaps include aspects of our behavior or personality that are known to others but not to ourselves.

Closing unconscious perception gaps is an important process that contributes to personal development and better understanding. In relation to sexualized violence, it becomes evident that individuals with unconscious perception gaps in this area can be respectfully made aware of their behavior and its impact through the PIW© method. This provides them with the opportunity to change their behavior.

On the other hand, closing perception gaps with W3© can also help uncover individuals who act strategically and deliberately. Even after applying PIW©, it is unlikely that consciously acting perpetrators will change their behavior. However, as affected individuals, witnesses, or those in leadership positions, you gain certainty by clearly addressing sexualized violence with PIW©.

If incidents recur, you can take additional measures, seek support, or consider internal reports and external complaints without fear of false accusations.
If unconscious perception gaps remain undiscovered, situations are perceived incompletely or distorted. We tend to interpret information in a way that aligns with our

preconceived opinions or assumptions, leading to biases, misjudgments, or false conclusions. However, to make well-informed (behavioral) decisions, we need the most complete picture of the situation possible.

Sometimes, however, we lack the resources to provide feedback using a method like PIW© - because our thoughts are elsewhere, because we are tired, or because we do not want to give feedback yet again.
And that is okay.

In Chapter 14, you will find additional methods that you can try and use instead—depending on your personality, the individual situation, and your situational capacity.

BEING AN ALLY: EVERYONE COUNTS

The tips listed on the previous pages apply not only to those affected but also to witnesses and colleagues. They, too, can seek support, receive help and advice, document and report incidents of sexualized violence. We can all contribute to combating sexualized violence in the workplace and bringing about positive change.

By being allies.

By courageously standing up for our rights.

By taking action when we are witnesses.

By insisting on respectful interaction.

Treating each other with respect means recognizing the boundaries and consent of others and avoiding inappropriate behavior or any form of discrimination. Allies are indispensable. Through their support, influence, and commitment, they play a key role in creating positive change. Allies who act as witnesses play a crucial role by providing information and evidence that help confirm incidents and hold perpetrators accountable. By using their privileges and opportunities, allies serve as positive and essential role models.

As an ally, you can:

Expand knowledge and understanding,

Raise awareness,

Increase visibility of issues,

Give the concerns of those affected additional weight and credibility,

Show empathy,

Encourage,

Spark discussions,

Launch information campaigns,

Share resources,

Create a supportive network,

Question existing systems and structures,

Expose discriminatory practices,

Advocate for consequences for perpetrators,

Demand and initiate change,

Break down barriers and build bridges,

Foster community and solidarity.

We can all address the issue of sexualized violence in the workplace and support those affected by taking their feelings and experiences seriously. This means listening openly without prejudice and giving those affected the space to share their experiences. Together, we can seek concrete help and respond sensitively and respectfully to the needs of those affected, allowing them to express themselves.

One way we can support those affected is by offering a safe space - an (emotional) environment where people feel secure and protected.

"I am here to listen if you want to talk about what happened. I won't interrupt or judge you. You can share as much or as little as you like, and if you want, I will try to help you."

We can actively seek help. We can reach out to the works council or HR together with the affected person. We can contact a counseling center and assist the affected person in finding professional help. We can ask them what kind of support they need and help them access it. We can ask open, non-judgmental questions:

"What can I do to support you?"

By doing this, we send a clear message:

You are not alone!" and "We are not alone!"

As a witness, you can act as an ally by:

Documenting incidents quickly and clearly
If you witness an incident of sexualized violence, document what you saw or heard as quickly and in as much detail as possible. Record the date, time, location, and people involved. This documentation is valuable information.

Remaining impartial
Ensure that your personal opinion does not influence your documentation or report. Your role is to present the facts objectively and impartially to enable a fair investigation.

Providing active support
Offer emotional support to those affected. Listen to them, show empathy, and make it clear that you stand by them. Your support is crucial for their well-being and decision-making.

Maintaining confidentiality
Handle all information you receive with the utmost confidentiality. Discretion is essential to maintaining the trust of those affected and protecting the integrity of the investigation.

Knowing guidelines and protocols
Familiarize yourself with the workplace policies and procedures regarding the reporting and handling of sexualized violence. Ensure that you know how and to whom incidents should be reported.

Facilitating access to resources
Help those affected access support services such as counseling, legal assistance, or medical care.

Acting ethically

Act ethically and responsibly. Avoid spreading speculation or unverified claims. The goal is to contribute to clarification and ensure fair and respectful treatment of all involved.

By not looking away in moments of suspicion but instead observing, listening, and taking action, we acknowledge the seriousness of incidents and situations. We can report them, stop them, or even prevent them. The role of an ally is invaluable. Your commitment and support are of immense importance and actively contribute to creating a fairer and violence-free culture.

Your stance as an ally not only strengthens those affected but also inspires others to advocate for positive change.

Be proud to be an ally!

CHAPTER 14

COMMUNICATION
CLEAR AND CONSTRUCTIVE

Effective communication skills are essential when it comes to identifying and ending sexualized violence in the workplace.

Communicating clearly and precisely is just as valuable as the use of nonverbal signals and paraverbal nuances.

This chapter shows how you can use verbal, nonverbal, and paraverbal communication intentionally to prevent violence in the workplace and which strategies are particularly effective in doing so.

VERBAL COMMUNICATION: YOUR WORDS

While verbal communication includes direct expressions such as words and sentences, nonverbal elements like body language and facial expressions play a crucial role in how messages are received and interpreted. Paraverbal communication, which involves tone of voice, volume, and pace of speech, can significantly influence the intentions behind our words.

By using these three dimensions of communication deliberately, we avoid misunderstandings and take action to defuse aggressive behaviors, fostering a safe work environment. You can directly address perpetrators:

"Stop!"

A direct and clear "Stop!" is an immediate response to inappropriate behavior by perpetrators and can prompt them to stop their actions. It signals that their behavior is considered unacceptable and will no longer be tolerated. A "Stop!" sets a vocal boundary and reminds perpetrators that their behavior is inappropriate and impermissible.

"I want you to stop harassing me."

This clear statement shows perpetrators that their behavior is unwanted and happening against your will. It also shows that you will not tolerate harassment and will assert your right to defend yourself against inappropriate behavior.

"Your behavior makes me uncomfortable. Stop it."

This sentence expresses your feelings and shows the perpetrator that their behavior has a negative impact on you. It encourages the perpetrator to become aware of the effect of their actions and urges them to change their inappropriate behavior.

"I don't understand what you meant by that. Can you explain it to me?"

This question confronts perpetrators with their own statements or behaviors. By asking them to explain their actions and words, they are forced to consciously engage with their statements, reflect on their behavior, and justify themselves.

"Do you know how I feel? Like this ..."

This sentence expresses your feelings directly and shows the perpetrator how their actions and words affect you. It confronts them with the emotional impact of their inappropriate behavior and may evoke understanding and empathy from the perpetrator.

"Stop staring at me and focus on the work!"

This request is revealing and signals that the displayed behavior is perceived as disturbing, inappropriate, and unproductive. By naming out loud what the person is doing and telling them what they should be doing instead, you set a clear boundary.

Reactions from perpetrators to such statements vary. Some perpetrators are receptive and change their behavior. This is particularly true for those who have never consciously considered their own behavior and its impact before. They may have made comments or gestures they thought were appropriate and normal. These are often individuals who lack awareness of the issue of sexualized violence or have unconscious gaps in perception. Such people frequently adjust their behavior afterward because they do not want to be perpetrators.

Other perpetrators respond defensively or aggressively. In such cases, unpleasant situations can quickly arise, and it is important to de-escalate the communication and ensure your safety. Such perpetrators often feel personally attacked and deny any responsibility for their behavior. They try to justify their actions or blame the victims. In such cases, it is crucial to stay calm and act thoughtfully. Remain factual and leave the situation. A respectful and professional attitude also helps defuse such situations while standing up for yourself.

Imagine you are in a meeting with several colleagues. A colleague, Mr. Schmidt, makes an inappropriate comment about your clothing by saying:

"The pants are quite daring for the office, aren't they?"

What does this sentence trigger in you? How would you ideally react? What suits you?
Select one or more of the following options with which you feel comfortable:

"No!"

With this clear answer, you set a distinct boundary – whether friendly or unfriendly. "No" is a complete sentence, and "No" does not require an explanation or justification.

"Pardon?"

This one-word sentence expresses irritation and disapproval. Depending on your tone and pitch, it can come across as sharp or questioning. Either way, it gives you time to prepare a further response.

"Could you repeat that, please?"

This polite or incredulous request can make the person reconsider their inappropriate behavior or remarks. It signals that you do not accept it and expect an explanation.

"You didn't just say that?!

This sentence shows outrage and disbelief at what was heard. It indirectly encourages the other person to reflect on their statement and become aware of its inappropriateness.

Why do you think it's okay to say something like that?"

This question forces the other person to rethink their behavior and justify it, which often leads them to realize how inappropriate it was.

Practice this whenever possible.

In every situation where you experience or witness inappropriate or harassing behavior – whether in the supermarket, on the street, talking to neighbors, or at work.

The more you practice, the more automated your reactions will become. You will feel increasingly confident. Eventually, it will no longer feel awkward, and you won't need to think about your response beforehand. Instead, you will act clearly, decisively, and confidently. Repetition strengthens your skills, so you can respond calmly and confidently even in challenging situations.

Perhaps you will also develop entirely different reactions that suit you. Be creative. What matters is that you regain control of the situation. How you do that is something you can decide individually for yourself.

NONVERBAL COMMUNICATION: YOUR POSTURE

You can additionally or solely use nonverbal signals to show that you feel uncomfortable and do not accept the displayed behavior. Nonverbal signals also emphasize what has been said and help prevent misunderstandings or insufficient expression of emotions.

Imagine you are at a company event, and a colleague makes inappropriate comments about your appearance. You feel uncomfortable and want to make this clear without words. Use one of the following behaviors – ideally, choose the one you feel confident and comfortable with:

Death Stare

Slowly turn towards the person and look them directly in the eyes with a gaze that could kill. In this way, you express your discomfort and disapproval without words, yet clearly and impressively, keeping others at a distance.

Demonstrative Ignorance

Cross your arms in front of your chest and slightly turn away from the person to signal your defensive posture. Alternatively, step back and/or slowly leave the room. This shows you are removing yourself from the situation and literally leaving, refusing to continue exposing yourself to the sexualized violence.

Power Pose

The Power Pose is a body posture that is often associated with a feeling of self-confidence, self-assurance, and dominance. It is an upright and open posture in which you present your body in a way that expresses strength and confidence. Typically, the Power Pose includes a straight body posture with an upright back and open shoulders. The arms hang either at the sides of the body, are placed on the hips, or are spread wide. The legs are slightly apart, and the feet are firmly placed on the ground. Your gaze is forward, and your facial expression is confident and determined! It conveys: Here I stand up for myself!

This posture is expansive and, therefore, boundary-setting. The Power Pose conveys your self-confidence and self-worth – simply because of the body posture. By adopting this pose, we feel more secure – physically and emotionally. Taking on a stable and upright posture creates a sense of strength and visibility. Both of these lead to increased self-awareness and a more positive mental state. Why the Power Pose works?

1. **The Nervous System Is Activated**
The Power Pose activates the parasympathetic nervous system, which is responsible for relaxation and recovery. This activation leads the body into a state of calmness and security. Through the upright and expansive posture, we feel less threatened.

2. **Hormones Are Released**
Studies have shown that adopting a Power Pose increases the production of testosterone, a hormone associated with power and self-assurance. At the same

time, the stress hormone cortisol is reduced. These hormonal changes contribute to a heightened sense of self-confidence and emotional stability.

3. Breathing Deepens
An upright and expansive posture improves chest opening and, therefore, breathing. Air can enter the lungs more deeply, leading to a calmer and deeper breath.

4. Neurological Effects Occur
The body's neural representation in the brain, particularly in the somatosensory cortex, is influenced by posture. An upright and extended posture leads to increased activation of brain areas associated with self-awareness and control. This enhances the perception of self-worth and self-efficacy.

5. Cognitive and Emotional Feedback Begins
An upright posture improves thought patterns and self-image. People in this pose often report a more positive self-perception and greater emotional resilience.

6. Social Perception Changes
The Power Pose not only affects your perception but also how others perceive you. An open, expansive posture signals confidence and authority, which can prompt corresponding reactions from others. This external feedback further strengthens the feeling of your own strength and self-assurance.

The effects of the Power Pose vary from person to person, and there is a lack of comprehensive scientific evidence for its universal effectiveness. Factors such as personal beliefs, individual experiences, and environmental influences determine how strongly the Power Pose works.

Despite these uncertainties, it is worth trying the Power Pose and seeing if it brings about a positive change in challenging situations.

Even though scientific proof is still lacking, consciously adopting a powerful and confident body posture can influence our self-perception and how we affect others.

Try the Power Pose before an important meeting, a challenging conversation, or in everyday life. Adopt a posture that exudes strength and self-assurance. Show yourself and others that you stand up for yourself and are aware of your own value. Perhaps this way, you will discover a new dimension of self-confidence and positive energy.

The International Hand Signal for Help[56]

Additionally, you can send a signal: the international hand signal for help with domestic and sexual violence by the Canadian Women's Foundation. To do this, raise your hand, fold your thumb in, and slowly curl the other fingers into a fist. Anyone who receives such a signal can discreetly make contact with the affected person, remove them from the perpetrators, and seek advice from contact persons, counseling centers, friends, supervisors, complaint offices, equality officers, works councils, security personnel, or the police.

Important Aspects of Nonverbal Reactions

If you do not use these to reinforce your verbal communication, please provide written or verbal feedback afterward, clearly and unambiguously stating your response to the situation you experienced.

Ideally, this should be done within 72 hours after the situation, as it will still be fresh in the short-term memory, making it easier for you and others involved to refer back to it.

PARAVERBAL COMMUNICATION: YOUR VOICE

Paraverbal communication refers to the way we speak. Tone, volume, speed, and emphasis. We can use these aspects to protect and restore our boundaries.

Firm Tone

Use a firm and determined tone to signal that the displayed behavior is unacceptable. Speak with a clear voice and avoid a hesitant or insecure tone.

Calm and Composed

Remain calm and as composed as possible while communicating your rejection. Avoid an excited or aggressive tone to prevent escalating the situation. A calm tone conveys authority and self-confidence.

Clear and Precise

Use clear language to convey your message precisely. Avoid vague or unclear expressions and use definite words.

Emphasizing Key Words

By emphasizing key words in your sentence structure, you reinforce and highlight your message. Communicate "I" statements and emphasize them.

Be mindful that your paraverbal communication is not perceived as aggressive or provocative, as this could escalate the situation. It is advisable to speak calmly and firmly to communicate your rejection clearly and distinctly. Practice and train your paraverbal strengths by, for example, using these formulations and emphases:

"I want you to stop harassing me immediately."

"I do not accept you speaking to me like that."

"This is not okay. I do not tolerate such behavior."

"Do you know how I feel because of your sexist jokes?"

WRITTEN COMMUNICATION: YOUR SENTENCES

The method of written communication can also be used afterward to respond and have proof that you clearly and explicitly communicated that the behavior shown to you (or others) is unwelcome.

"Dear [Name], I am writing to inform you that I find the behavior you displayed in the following situation inappropriate and will no longer tolerate it. I expect you to stop immediately."

By E-Mail

You can send an email to the relevant person and clearly express that the displayed behavior is unacceptable to you and/or the company.

By Letter

You can write a letter to express your rejection. A letter also provides the opportunity to speak in detail and extensively.

By SMS or WhatsApp

Communication via SMS or WhatsApp is not always recommended. Both forms of communication appear more informal and colloquial, which leads to a less professional and respectful atmosphere. SMS and

WhatsApp are also quick and easy to send, so senders may respond impulsively and thoughtlessly, which could lead to escalation or insufficient confrontation. In the event of a legal dispute or further intensification of the situation, it is often difficult to use SMS or WhatsApp messages as evidence. Written communication by email or letter, on the other hand, offers verifiable proof.

Make sure that your message is clear and that the expectations regarding the displayed behavior are clearly formulated. Use PIW©. Avoid offensive or provocative language and remain factual. Choose the form of communication and language that works best for you and feels the safest.

Sometimes, it may be necessary or supportive for you to seek help from trusted individuals, supervisors, or professionals. It is okay and even important to seek support and find solutions and strategies together.

Always prioritize your safety. There is no universal way to respond to sexualized violence. However, every person has the right to protect themselves from harassing behavior and set clear boundaries. What matters is that you react.

DOCUMENTATION:
YOUR THOUGHTS AS A MEMORY AID

Keeping a memory log for documentation supports your self-efficacy and boundary-setting. Document all incidents of sexualized violence so that you have your records on hand when you need evidence or references. Logs and documentation serve various functions:

1. Evidence
A detailed documentation of incidents serves as important evidence if legal action, complaints, or procedures are required. By recording the date, time, place, witnesses, and details of the incident in a memory log, you create a record that validates your experiences and encounters, should this be needed.

2. Clarity and Accuracy
Documentation helps you record incidents clearly and accurately, so you can later recall the details more precisely. Human memory can become inaccurate over time, so it's important to document events as soon as possible after they occur to ensure the accuracy of the information.

3. Support for Complaints
If you decide to file a complaint about the sexualized violence incident, detailed documentation will support your report. You can refer to your memory log as a reference and use the information to clarify your concerns and issues.

4. Emotional Protection
Maintaining a memory log helps protect your emotional health. It is stressful to experience or talk about incidents

of sexualized violence. Documentation assists in processing and sorting your thoughts and emotions.

With documentation, you protect your safety. To avoid making yourself vulnerable, refrain from using real names or other personal information of witnesses or involved parties, unless you have explicit consent to do so.
Equally important and correct is informing your employer, the company's complaints office, the equality officer, and the works or staff council. Report incidents of sexualized violence as soon as you are ready. There is no "too late" or "too early" emotionally.

On the contrary:
It is important to report incidents when you feel secure doing so, for many reasons. However, keep in mind the currently valid reporting deadline of two months after an incident so that appropriate (legal) measures can be taken:

Protection from Further Incidents
Reporting incidents of sexualized violence in the workplace helps prevent further occurrences. After reporting, employers must take appropriate measures to ensure the safety and well-being of those affected and other employees.

Legal and Employment Law Actions
Employers, company complaint offices, equality officers, or works or staff councils can take employment law measures after a report, provide support and advice, and take appropriate steps to clarify the incident and enforce the rights of those affected.

Creating a Safe Working Environment
Reporting incidents of sexualized violence contributes to creating a safe working environment. It is important for employers to receive such reports and be able to take appropriate actions to ensure the safety and well-being of the workforce.

Support for Those Affected
Reporting incidents of sexualized violence provides sustainable support for those affected. It helps in the long run by ensuring that they are heard, taken seriously, and gain access to support services, counseling, or other resources that help them cope with the emotional, psychological, and legal impacts of the incident.

Reporting incidents of sexualized violence in the workplace benefits not only those affected but all employees and the overall work environment.
It contributes in the long term to creating a positive working environment where sexualized violence is not tolerated and everyone works together respectfully and safely.

If - yes, if - employers handle these reports carefully, sensitively, and seriously!

If your company or contact persons do not do this or you fear that they will not, seek external support.
There are many external organizations that offer support and counseling. Use these resources as they provide a wide range of help:

Independent and Neutral Counseling
External organizations offer independent and neutral counseling. They assist in assessing the situation, clarifying rights and options, and developing strategies for action without being influenced by internal company interests.

Specialized Expertise
External organizations often have specialized expertise in sexualized violence. They draw on experience and resources to provide the best possible support tailored to the individual situation.

Anonymity and Confidentiality
Approaching an external organization offers the advantage of anonymity and confidentiality. This is especially important if you are concerned about potential effects on your career or working relationships.

Additional Support Options
External organizations highlight additional support options, such as psychological counseling, legal consultations, or assistance in initiating legal steps.

Strengthening Your Rights
Using external support helps you enforce your rights and handle the situation with confidence. With the help of external organizations, you can make more informed decisions.

You can find the first points of contact under "Important Contacts" at the end of this book.

CHAPTER 15

RESOURCES
PATHS TO HEALING

Sexualized violence at the workplace can be and often is traumatic and burdensome for those affected and other involved parties.

It is therefore important to know that there are support services that can help cope with the effects, find healing, and protect one's rights.

Various therapeutic approaches support dealing with the emotional and psychological consequences of experiences of sexualized violence at the workplace.

THERAPEUTIC APPROACHES: TRAUMA AND COPING

Experiencing sexualized violence can lead to trauma. Trauma is a profound emotional reaction to an extremely distressing or painful event, which exceeds the normal processing of experiences.

Professional therapists provide support in treating trauma-related disorders, such as post-traumatic stress disorder (PTSD), depression, anxiety, and other psychological symptoms, through various approaches:

Cognitive Behavioral Therapy (CBT)
In cognitive behavioral therapy, the thoughts, feelings, and behavior patterns of those affected in relation to the trauma are identified and changed. This approach helps to recognize negative thought patterns and behaviors to better cope with the effects of trauma.

Eye Movement Desensitization and Reprocessing (EMDR)
EMDR is a specialized form of therapy aimed at improving memory processing. It uses eye movements or other forms of bilateral stimulation to support the processing of traumatic experiences and to deal with distressing memories.

Art and Body Therapy
These therapeutic approaches use creative forms of expression such as art, music, or movement to help those affected cope with their feelings and experiences.

Trauma-Focused Psychotherapy
This approach focuses on the adaptation of traumatic

experiences using techniques specifically aimed at trauma processing to reduce symptoms and change emotional experiences. This is done by developing safe memory frameworks and confronting anxiety symptoms in a protected environment.

Somatic Experiencing
Somatic Experiencing is a body-focused therapy that centers on physical responses to trauma. This approach regulates the impact of trauma on the nervous system by focusing on physical sensations and their relaxation. Through this method, those affected learn to reduce traumatic stress reactions and feel safer in their own bodies.

Systemic Therapy
Systemic therapy does not view problems in isolation but in the context of relationships and the environment of those affected. This form of therapy is helpful in understanding the impact of trauma in a social context and mobilizing support through the social network. It helps identify and change dysfunctional patterns.

Acceptance and Commitment Therapy (ACT)
ACT is based on the idea that accepting one's thoughts and feelings, as well as committing to personal values, leads to a more fulfilling life. This approach helps to distance oneself from distressing thoughts and feelings and to focus on living according to one's values. ACT reduces the emotional burden of trauma by focusing on positive change.

These methods, depending on individual needs and symptoms, may be combined or used separately to provide comprehensive support and therapy. Professional therapeutic support from specialized experts is recommended, as it is a crucial step in dealing with the effects of sexualized violence and restoring health and well-being.

You can access therapeutic services in your area through local counseling centers, your health insurance company, or the regional medical associations.

SELF-HELP:
EMPOWERMENT AND STRENGTHENING

Self-help groups provide the opportunity to exchange with others affected, share feelings, and support each other. They serve as safe spaces where those affected can speak about their experiences without fear of judgment or stigma. Through exchange, they encourage each other, develop empowerment strategies, and find new ways to cope with their experiences of violence. This often leads to improved mental health and enhanced self-esteem of the participants, who learn to express their own needs better and stand up for their rights.

Self-help toolkits, online guides, and materials for those affected by sexualized violence are also important resources on the path to coping and healing. They offer information, practical tips, and exercises that are practical and usable in daily life.

Additionally, (specialized) literature offers numerous ideas to strengthen self-help and empowerment abilities. Books by survivors or experts on the topic serve as valuable impulses to gain information, perspectives, and practical guidance.

All of these approaches complement professional help. Every person has different needs, and what works for one person may not necessarily work for another. Try different methods and encourage others to do the same.

SELF-CARE:
AFTER EXPERIENCES

After experiences of sexualized violence, it is more than important to care for ourselves. To strengthen, encourage, and love ourselves. Even as an ally, it is important to take space for our feelings, thoughts, and self-care. We can do this by:

Creating Safe Environments
When we find ourselves in a threatening or unsafe situation, we should remove ourselves and find a safe space. This could be a trusted place, a protected room, or the contact with someone we feel comfortable and safe with.

Seeking Conversations
Talking about what we've experienced brings relief. By sharing our experiences, perceptions, and worries, we alleviate emotional burdens and protect ourselves. Sharing experiences helps process our feelings and allows us to gain new perspectives and advice from others.

Supporting each other and offering encouragement
strengthens us and fosters community and connection. This social support contributes to improving our well-being and reduces the feeling of isolation.

Gathering Information
Knowledge provides us with certainty and helps us plan the next steps with focus and make informed decisions about what support or resources are needed. Additionally, it enables a proactive approach to challenges and encourages goal-oriented action.

Using Stabilizing Factors

Consider which stabilizing and supportive factors are available to you. These could be self-care strategies, relaxation, or routines that stabilize your emotional balance.

Developing Personal Coping Strategies

Use healthy ways of managing stress, such as physical activity, meditation, mindfulness exercises, or creative forms of expression such as painting, writing, or music. Do what feels good to you! Pay attention to regular breaks and sufficient sleep to ensure proper recovery. Set realistic goals and plan your steps. This way, you stay focused and motivated even when challenges arise. Stay open to change and be flexible in dealing with new situations. Adaptability is key to handling challenges.

Replacing Negative Thoughts with Positive Ones

Self-talk helps maintain a healthy self-perception and stay optimistic. Even if it may seem unusual at first, positive self-talk contributes to your emotional well-being. By encouraging yourself and emphasizing your strengths, you build self-confidence and create a mental attitude that supports you in challenging situations. Often, small changes can lead to significant positive transformations.

Combine these building blocks and create safety in uncertain and stressful situations.

LEGAL OPTIONS: CONTACT POINTS

Those affected by sexualized violence at the workplace receive legal protection and support through various contact points and organizations:

Lawyers
Lawyers, especially those with experience in labor law and victim protection, can assist those affected with the legal processing of incidents, such as reporting the case, enforcing compensation claims, or filing lawsuits.

Unions
Unions support those affected by sexualized violence at the workplace in matters of labor law and victim protection. They provide information on the rights and obligations of employees and help enforce claims. Unions also include reports of such incidents in their own statistics, if available, and initiate further steps to address systemic issues and promote improvements at the workplace.

Women's and Victim Counseling Centers
Specialized centers provide support and counseling specifically for those affected by sexualized violence. They provide information on legal options and assist those affected with filing reports and other legal proceedings.

Specialized Legal Counseling Centers for Sexualized
Violence at the Workplace
There are specialized legal counseling centers focused on cases of sexualized violence at the workplace and assist those affected in legal matters.

Local contact details for these support services vary by region. In addition to the contact points listed at the end of this book under "Important Contacts," research local resources and counseling centers in your area to find suitable contacts.

All the resources presented in this chapter - from therapeutic approaches to legal help, to self-help and self-care - are of great importance and complement each other. It is essential that you have access to a variety of support services and use them to receive comprehensive support. The contact details for support services may vary by region.

In addition to the contact points listed at the end of this book under "Important Contacts," research local resources and counseling centers in your area. These provide tailored help and strengthen you in finding and following your personal path to healing.

CHAPTER 16

THE VISION
A VIOLENCE-FREE WORKPLACE

Sexualized violence in the workplace is destructive and leads to significant losses, as the previous chapters have shown.

In contrast, ending sexualized violence in the workplace brings great benefits and added value—both for companies and for the people working for and with them.

Because once again: a safe working environment promotes a sense of unity, productivity, stability, and the success of all!

WHAT DO WE LOSE...
IF WE DO NOT END SEXUALIZED VIOLENCE IN THE WORKPLACE?

The effects of sexualized violence in the workplace are devastating if not addressed and fought against. And we lose a lot:

Affected individuals and witnesses lose their health, their careers, their self-worth
They often suffer from profound negative emotional impacts, which lead to a decline in their quality of life and work performance. Their careers are at risk, and their self-esteem is undermined, leading to long-term social isolation and personal misery.

Companies lose their constructive working atmosphere, integrity, and reputation
Instead of a healthy, productive working environment, a toxic culture of distrust and fear thrives. The company's reputation is damaged. The reputational damage leads to a massive loss of trust in the company, its stakeholders, and its competitiveness.

As a society, we lose justice, progress, and prosperity
Social injustices increase, societal progress is slowed down, economic and social costs rise, and the culture of solidarity is severely disrupted.

If we do not fight sexualized violence decisively, we pay a high price.

WHAT DO WE GAIN...
IF WE END SEXUALIZED VIOLENCE IN THE
WORKPLACE?

If we fight and stop sexualized violence in the workplace decisively, we gain:

Affected individuals and witnesses gain health, career opportunities, and self-worth
As the fear and trauma fade, they can focus fully on their tasks, advance their careers, and build strong self-esteem. Support and safety foster a fulfilling, productive work life, contributing to social and professional integration.

Companies gain a healthy working atmosphere, integrity, and reputation
With sexualized violence ended, a constructive, trust-based atmosphere is created. Companies enhance their integrity and reputation, boosting productivity, reducing turnover, and attracting talent. This ensures long-term success for the company and its employees.

As a society, we gain justice, progress, and economic prosperity
Eliminating sexualized violence promotes a just, non-violent society where everyone has equal opportunities. This reduces health and social costs, strengthens economic productivity, and fosters a culture of solidarity, increasing social cohesion and overall prosperity.

And the encouraging thing about it:

Every action counts.

CONCLUSION & ENCOURAGEMENT

As a society, as companies, and as individuals, we are responsible for creating a safe, fair, and respectful working environment.

Sexualized violence in the workplace is absolutely unacceptable. Together, we can make a meaningful difference and actively take action against it.

Because we are not alone. We are many.

We can support, encourage, and accompany each other. Through awareness, attentive observation, listening, and decisive action, we create a strong and respectful community. It is up to us to be role models, multipliers, and allies - no matter what role or function we have in the workplace.

We can reflect on our own thoughts and behaviors and actively stand against inappropriate conduct, learned prejudices, and demeaning communication.
Together, we establish and live a culture of respect, appreciation, and equality. We drive change forward and enable a future where sexualized violence in the workplace belongs to the past. We are determined to create a working environment where every person is safe, valued, and respected.

By seeing, naming and stoping sexualized violence!

IMPORTANT CONTACTS

These services provide anonymous, confidential, competent, and mostly free support.

AUSTRALIA

Fair Work Commission
1300 799 675 & www.fwc.gov.au

Australian Human Rights Commission
1300 656 419 & www.humanrights.gov.au

AUSTRIA

Telefonseelsorge
142 & www.telefonseelsorge.at

Opfer Notruf
0800 112 112 & www.opfer-notruf.at

CANADA

Canadian Human Rights Commission (CHRC)
1-888-214-1090 & www.chrc-ccdp.gc.ca

Ending Violence Association of Canada
www.endviolencecanada.org

EUROPEAN UNION

European Institute for Gender Equality (EIGE)
+370 5 215 7440 & www.eige.europa.eu

The Group of Experts on Action against Violence against Women and Domestic Violence (GREVIO)
+33 3 88 41 20 00 & www.coe.int

GERMANY

Antidiskriminierungsstelle des Bundes
0800 546 5465 & www.antidiskriminierungsstelle.de

Hilfetelefon
116 016 & www.hilfetelefon.de

SOUTH AFRICA

The Commission for Gender Equality (CGE)
011 403 7189 & www.cge.org.za

Sexual Violence Research Initiative
www.svri.org

SWITZERLAND

Opferhilfe
www.opferhilfe-schweiz.ch/de/

UNITED KINGDOM

Equality and Human Rights Commission
0808 800 0082 & www.equalityhumanrights.com

The Survivors Trust
0845 122 8687 & www.thesurvivorstrust.org

UNITED STATES

Equal Employment Opportunity Commission (EEOC)
1-800-669-4000 & www.eeoc.gov

RAINN (Rape, Abuse & Incest National Network)
1-800-656-HOPE & www.rainn.org

You can get in touch with organizations offering support for victims of sexualized violence worldwide through the following websites:

The Global Network of Women's Shelters
www.womenshelters.org

United Nations Women
www.unwomen.org

SafeHorizon
www.safehorizon.org

Rape Crisis Network Europe
www.rcne.com

SOURCES

All listed sources were last accessed online on April 4th, 2025.

[1] https://zms.bundeswehr.de/resource/blob/5323764/1fd7d34f7236cc2b-b9200ae901e92cf4/studie-tabu-und-tolerenz-data.pdf

[2] https://www.antidiskriminierungsstelle.de/DE/ueber-diskriminierung/diskriminierungsmerkmale/sexuelle-identitaet/paragraph_175/paragraph_175_node.html

[3] https://www.thelavenderscare.com/

[4] https://www.gesetze-im-internet.de/agg/

[5] https://www.antidiskriminierungsstelle.de/SharedDocs/downloads/DE/publikationen/Expertisen/umgang_mit_sexueller_belaestigung_am_arbeitsplatz_kurzfassung.pdf?__blob=publicationFile&v=11

[6] https://www.ufo-online.aero/images/themen/gesundheit/pdf/umfrage_sexuelle_belaestigung.pdf?_t=1557477747

[7] https://bjs.ojp.gov/content/pub/pdf/cv20sst.pdf

[8] https://www.destatis.de/DE/Themen/Arbeit/Verdienste/Verdienste-Gender-PayGap/_inhalt.html#

[9] https://www.bka.de/DE/AktuelleInformationen/StatistikenLagebilder/PolizeilicheKriminalstatistik/PKS2019/PKSTabellen/Zeitreihen/zeitreihen_node.html

[10] https://www.i-p-bm.com/images/Literatur_und_Presse/stalking_arbeitsmedizin.pdf

[11] https://www.destatis.de/DE/Presse/Pressemitteilungen/2024/03/PD24_083_621.html

[12] https://ecamaastricht.org/blueandyellow-zoomingin/equal-pay-in-europe-where-does-the-gender-pay-gap-stand-in-2024?utm_source=chatgpt.com

[13] https://elpais.com/opinion/2025-03-06/la-paradoja-del-talento-el-coste-economico-de-la-brecha-de-genero.html?utm_source=chatgpt.com

[14] https://www.destatis.de/DE/Themen/Arbeit/Arbeitsmarkt/Qualitaet-Arbeit/Dimension-1/frauen-fuehrungspositionen.html

15 https://www.reederverband.de/sites/default/files/publikationen/deutsche_-seeschifffahrt/deutsche_seeschifffahrt_-_ausgabe_q4-2020.pdf

16 https://www.weforum.org/reports/gender-gap-2020-report-100-years-pay-equality/

17 https://iqb.de/karrieremagazin/mint/frauen-in-mint-berufen-und-studien-gaengen

18 https://eige.europa.eu/sites/default/files/documents/20204159_mh0220657-den_pdf.pdf

19 https://crashstats.nhtsa.dot.gov/Api/Public/ViewPublication/813358, zuletzt abgerufen am 12.06.2023

20 vfa-Positionspapier, Berücksichtigung von Frauen und Männern bei der Arzneimittelforschung, Februar 2023

21 https://www.gesetze-im-internet.de/agg/

22 https://www.bmfsfj.de/resource/blob/140386/59a79b46512d-feaa23af3d8906768679/sexuelle-belaestigung-im-job-data.pdf

23 https://weisser-ring.de/pm_sexualisierte_gewalt#:~:text=Alle acht Minuten wird ein,gegen die sexuelle Selbstbestimmung festhält.

24 https://ec.europa.eu/eurostat/web/gender-based-violence/database

25 https://www.ilo.org/sites/default/files/wcmsp5/groups/public/@dgreports/@dcomm/documents/publication/wcms_863095.pdf

26 https://www.antidiskriminierungsstelle.de/SharedDocs/downloads/DE/publikationen/Expertisen/umgang_mit_sexueller_belaestigung_am_arbeitsplatz_kurzfassung.pdf?__blob=publicationFile&v=11

27 https://www.antidiskriminierungsstelle.de/SharedDocs/downloads/DE/publikationen/Leitfaeden/leitfaden_was_tun_bei_sexueller_belaestigung.pdf?__blob=publicationFile&v=19

28 https://www.antidiskriminierungsstelle.de/SharedDocs/downloads/DE/publikationen/Leitfaeden/leitfaden_was_tun_bei_sexueller_belaestigung.pdf?__blob=publicationFile&v=19

29 https://www.antidiskriminierungsstelle.de/SharedDocs/forschungsprojekte/DE/UMFRAGE_sex_Belaestigung_am_ArbPlatz.html?nn=305536#bodyText

30 https://www.dbb.de/fileadmin/user_upload/globale_elemente/pdfs/2018/for-sa_2018.pdf

31 https://www.antidiskriminierungsstelle.de/SharedDocs/downloads/DE/publikationen/Leitfaeden/leitfaden_was_tun_bei_sexueller_belaestigung.pdf?__blob=publicationFile&v=19

32 https://www.bmfsfj.de/resource/blob/140386/59a79b46512d-feaa23af3d8906768679/sexuelle-belaestigung-im-job-data.pdf

33 https://www.antidiskriminierungsstelle.de/SharedDocs/downloads/DE/publikationen/Expertisen/umgang_mit_sexueller_belaestigung_am_arbeitsplatz.html

34 https://www.bmfsfj.de/resource/blob/140386/59a79b46512d-feaa23af3d8906768679/sexuelle-belaestigung-im-job-data.pdf

35 https://feps-europe.eu/wp-content/uploads/downloads/publications/survey sexism and sexual harassment at work feps fjj 2019_en .pdf

36 https://www.bgw-online.de/resource/blob/22160/5d35353fe4c9037e6a-e64a010e796808/bericht-gewalt-pflege-data.pdf

37 https://eige.europa.eu/publications-resources/publications/costs-gender-based-violence-european-union

38 https://www.etuc.org/sites/default/files/document/files/final_report_de_0.docx&psig=AOvVaw1Chjt9ZdTyw7jVsnjonQ3Y&ust=1686045765544579

39 https://www.bmz.de/de/themen/frauenrechte-und-gender/frauen-staerkung-wirtschaftliche-teilhabe

40 https://www.gesetze-im-internet.de/agg/index.html#BJNR189710006BJNE000100000

41 https://blogs.lse.ac.uk/businessreview/2019/01/29/the-flip-side-of-segregation-men-in-typically-female-jobs/

42 Zero Tolerance Report, 2019, Europäischen Föderation der Gewerkschaften in den Sektoren Lebensmittel, (EFFAT) im Rahmen eines von der Europäischen Union kofinanzierten Projekts Finanzhilfevereinbarung VS/2019/0035

43 The costs of gender-based violence in the European Union , 2021, European Institute for Gender Equality, 2021

44 The economic costs of sexual harassment in the workplace, Final Report 2019, Deloitte Access Economics Pty Ltd

45 Paying Today and Tomorrow, Charting the Financial Costs of Workplace Sexual Harassment, Ariane Hegewisch, Jessica Forden, and Eve Mefferd, July 2021, Institute for Women's Policy Research and the TIME'S UP™ Foundation

46 https://www.bmz.de/de/themen/frauenrechte-und-gender/frauen-staerkung-wirtschaftliche-teilhabe

47 https://feps-europe.eu/wp-content/uploads/downloads/publications/116268_rapport_feps-fjj_uk.pdf

48 https://www.lexology.com/library/detail.aspx?g=5ab39cb3-f3ac-4981-b444-1ddb1d1dd7d0

49 https://de.statista.com/statistik/daten/studie/1100866/umfrage/rangliste-der-eu-laender-nach-geschlechtsspezifischer-ungleichheit-im-gender-inequality-index/

50 https://de.statista.com/statistik/daten/studie/1098311/umfrage/frauenanteil-in-fuehrungspositionen-in-der-eu/

51 https://www.ipu.org/resources/publications/issue-briefs/2018-10/sexism-harassment-and-violence-against-women-in-parliaments-in-europe

52 https://www.ipsos.com/sites/default/files/ct/news/documents/2023-03/Ipsos-PI_Weltfrauentag_2023-03-07.pdf

53 https://www.researchgate.net/profile/Gerd-Bohner/publication/305722966_-Falschbeschuldigungen_bei_sexueller_Gewalt_False_allegations_of_sexual_violence/links/64c65eff5c44f86be6d5477e/Falschbeschuldigungen-bei-sexueller-Gewalt-False-allegations-of-sexual-violence.pdf

54 https://www.antidiskriminierungsstelle.de/SharedDocs/downloads/DE/Sonstiges/20230718_AGG_Reform.pdf?__blob=publicationFile&v=12

55 Effective gender equality training: analysing the preconditions and success factors, 2014, European Institute for Gender Equality

56 https://signalresponder.ca